UNIVERSITY OF NORTH CAROLINA AT CHAPEL HILL
DEPARTMENT OF ROMANCE LANGUAGES

NORTH CAROLINA STUDIES
IN THE ROMANCE LANGUAGES AND LITERATURES

Founder: URBAN TIGNER HOLMES

Distributed by:

UNIVERSITY OF NORTH CAROLINA PRESS
CHAPEL HILL
North Carolina 27514
U.S.A.

NORTH CAROLINA STUDIES IN THE
ROMANCE LANGUAGES AND LITERATURES
Number 216

THE INSTRUCTIONS OF SAINT LOUIS:
A CRITICAL TEXT

THE INSTRUCTIONS OF SAINT LOUIS:
A CRITICAL TEXT

BY

DAVID O'CONNELL

CHAPEL HILL

NORTH CAROLINA STUDIES IN THE ROMANCE
LANGUAGES AND LITERATURES
U.N.C. DEPARTMENT OF ROMANCE LANGUAGES
1979

Library of Congress Cataloging in Publication Data

O'Connell, David.
  The instructions of Saint Louis.

  (North Carolina studies in the Romance languages and literatures; no 216)
  Includes text of the manuscript of St. Louis' instructions to his daughter, the Lady Isabelle.

  Bibliography: p.
  1. Louis IX, Saint, King of France, 1214-1270. 2. France—History—Louis IX, 1226-1270. I. Louis IX, Saint, King of France, 1214-1270. II. Isabelle, Queen of Navarre, 1242-1271. III. Title. IV. Series.

DC91.A2032   248'.48'2   79-21276
ISBN 0-8078-9216-5

I. S. B. N. 0-8078-9216-5

DEPÓSITO LEGAL: V. 2.925 - 1979   I.S.B.N. 84-499-3334-X
ARTES GRÁFICAS SOLER, S. A. - OLIVERETA, 28 - VALENCIA (18) - 1979

This book has been published with the aid of funds awarded by the Faculty Research Council of the University of Massachusetts, Amherst.

Mānibus uxoris
carissimae sacratum.

Cathleen Casey O'Connell
1945-1978

LIST OF ABBREVIATIONS

ABSHF	Annuaire-Bulletin de la Société de l'Histoire de France
BECh	Bibliothèque de l'Ecole des Chartes
BSHF	Bulletin de la Société de l'Histoire de France
HLF	Histoire Littéraire de la France
RHGF	Recueil des Historiens des Gaules et de la France

TABLE OF CONTENTS

	Page
Introduction	15
Chapter	
I. The Manuscripts of the Instructions	17
II. Medieval Testimony	20
III. Critical Controversy	30
IV. Textual Analysis	37
V. Date, Sources and Structure of the Instructions.	56
VI. The Instructions to Isabelle	75
Appendix: Two Forged Texts of the Instructions	86
Bibliography	100

INTRODUCTION

When Jean de Joinville presented his *Histoire de Saint Louis* to the future Louis X [1] in 1309, the manuscript he offered to Saint Louis' great-grandson contained a copy of the *Enseignements* that Louis IX (1226-1270) had written a few years before his death for his son and successor, the future Philip the Bold (1270-1285). Joinville's *Histoire* did not contain, however, a copy of the *Enseignements* that the king had written for his oldest daughter, Isabelle, Countess of Champagne and Queen of Navarre. Interestingly, just as the inclusion of the *Enseignements à Philippe* in Joinville's *Histoire* has brought to that text of Saint Louis a relatively wide readership over the last six and a half centuries, the inverse has been true of the *Enseignements à Isabelle*. Their original omission from Joinville's *Histoire de Saint Louis* has helped to make them less well known, but in our opinion they are still no less important than the *Enseignements à Philippe*.

Over the last century, but especially since the appearance in 1867 of Natalis de Wailly's first modern critical edition of Joinville's *Histoire*, [2] a degree of doubt and uncertainty has continued to exist with regard to the authenticity of the two sets of *Enseignements* written by Saint Louis for his two oldest children. In our previous study, the *Teachings of Saint Louis*, [3] we attempted to settle

---

[1] Louis X (1289-1316), son of Philip the Fair (1285-1314), was King of France (1314-1316) and King of Navarre (1305-1316).

[2] Jean de Joinville, *Histoire de Saint Louis, Credo et Lettre à Louis X, texte original, accompagné d'une traduction*, par M. Natalis de Wailly (Paris: Firmin-Didot, 1874). The first edition of the *Histoire* under the above title appeared in 1867. It was only in the 1874 edition, however, that de Wailly divided the text into numbered paragraphs.

[3] *The Teachings of Saint Louis: A Critical Text* (Chapel Hill: University of North Carolina Press, 1972).

the critical and textual problems relating to the text of the *Enseignements de Saint Louis à son fils Philippe*. In the present work, it is our goal to do the same for the *Enseignements à Isabelle*. For the sake of clarity, however, we shall refer in English to these *Enseignements à Isabelle* as the "Instructions to Isabelle" so as not to confuse them with the "Teachings to Philip."

Our immediate aim is to furnish a critical text of the Instructions based on a detailed study of all available manuscripts and printed editions of the work. In addition, we shall also attempt here to date the text, relate it to its possible sources, and analyze its structure. Elsewhere, in our book *Les Propos de Saint Louis*,[4] we have considered the Instructions, taken as a 13th century didactic text, in relation to the Teachings to Philip and to all of Louis' *propos*. The present work, which logically and philologically should have been published before *Les Propos de Saint Louis*, has had its appearance in print delayed for a number of reasons which need not be enumerated here. Despite this fact, it is offered now as a companion monograph to *The Teachings of Saint Louis* and as a partial underpinning for *Les Propos de Saint Louis*.

Special thanks in the preparation of this text go to Professor Alfred Foulet, Professor Emeritus of Princeton University, who read and commented on it as it was being written. No student ever owed more to a mentor than I to him. I am also indebted to Mrs. Ute Bargmann of the Interlibrary Loan Department of the University of Massachusetts Library for her tireless pursuit of rare texts and volumes. Also, this work would not have been possible without the generous support of the Faculty Research Council of the University of Massachusetts, Amherst. The Council's continuous and faithful support of my work over the years is gratefully acknowledged. Finally, my greatest debt is to my late wife. Without her loving support, this study would never have been completed.

---

[4] *Les Propos de Saint Louis*, préfacés par Jacques Le Goff (Paris: Gallimard, 1974).

CHAPTER I

THE MANUSCRIPTS OF THE INSTRUCTIONS

There are two separate manuscript families of the Instructions to Isabelle, one of which is Latinized and attributable to Guillaume de Saint-Pathus and the other written in a purer brand of Old French.

1. The extant texts of the Latinized version are:
A. B.N. ms. fr. 4976, fol. 97-213.
B. B.N. ms. fr. 5722, fol. 90-208v.
C. B.N. ms. fr. 5716, pp. 285-666.
D. Berlin, Deutsche Staatsbibliothek der DDR, Hamilton 412, fol. 91-102.

Each of these texts was composed after 1300. According to the studies made of the texts by H.-Fr. Delaborde and P. B. Fay,[1] we can make the following assertions about their respective dates cf composition. B.N. ms. fr. 4976 dates from the first quarter of the 14th century.[2] B.N. ms. fr. 5722, which dates from the first half of the 14th century, and B.N. ms. fr. 5716, which was made in the third quarter of the 14th century, are copies of B.N. ms. fr. 4976.[3] The

---

[1] Guillaume de Saint-Pathus, *Vie de Saint Louis*, éd. H.-François Delaborde (Paris: Picard, 1899), and Guillaume de Saint-Pathus, *Les Miracles de Saint Louis*, éd. Perceval B. Fay (Paris: Champion, 1931).
[2] Delaborde, p. XV; Fay, p. III.
[3] Delaborde, pp. XVII-XX; Fay, pp. V-VI. It ought to be noted that both editors take pains to explain that B.N. ms. fr. 4976 went through three successive stages of development which they refer to as A, A² and A³. The final form of this text, that of A³, seems to have been the major source of B, C and D.

Berlin text, unknown to Delaborde, also derives from B.N. ms. fr. 4976, and is dated by Fay at the end of the 14th or early part of the 15th century.

The text established by Delaborde appeared in:

E. *Vie de Saint Louis par Guillaume de Saint-Pathus, confesseur de la reine Marguerite*, ed. H.-François Delaborde, Paris, Picard, 1899, 59-63. It is based on the text contained in B.N. ms. fr. 4976.

Another printed text, based on B.N. 5722 (formerly ms. 10311A of the Bibliothèque Royale), can be found in:

F. *Recueil des Historiens des Gaules et de la France (RHGF)*, ed. Bouquet, XX (1840), 82-3.

2. The texts of the non-Latinized version are:

G. B. N. ms. fr. 25462, fol. 202r.-204v., which dates from about 1300.[4] The scribe of G wrote in a *picard* dialect, thereby slightly deforming the presumably *françien* holograph of Saint Louis. Thus, for example, he writes *chou* for *ce* and *cose* for *chose*.

H. A printed text of either G or of a text closely related to it, written in a *picard* dialect, which can be found appended to Jean de Joinville, *Vie de Saint Louis*, ed. Claude Ménard, Paris, 1617, pp. 356-9.[5]

I. This text published by Ménard has been reprinted in *Recueil des Historiens des Gaules et de la France*, XX, 302.

J. A modern French text, based on both G and B, and which in fact modernizes F, was published by Paul Viollet in *Oeuvres chrétiennes des familles royales de France*, Paris, Poussielgue, 1870, pp. 98-105.

K. The text discovered by Gérard de Montaigu in 1374 and which is now held by the Bibliothèque Municipale d'Amiens, Registre AA4, fol. 173r.-174v. André Artonne, with whose judgment

---

[4] See Paul Viollet, "Note sur le véritable texte des Instructions de Saint Louis à sa fille et à son fils Philippe le Hardi," *Bibliothèque de l'Ecole des Chartes*, (*BECh*), XXX (1869), 129-48. See especially pp. 130 and 134.

[5] A copy of this rare volume is currently held by the library of the University of Minnesota.

we agree, has dated this text "à la fin du XVe siècle, au règne de Charles VIII ou de Louis XII." [6]

L. The text discovered by Montaigu has been rather carelessly transcribed by H. Dusevel in *Bulletin de la Société de l'Histoire de France (BSHF)*, 2 août 1841, 128-30. [7]

M. B.N. ms. fr. 22921, fol. 239r.-241r., which dates from the 14th century.

N. B.N. ms. fr. 916, fol. 140r.-141v., which dates from the 14th century. [8]

---

[6] André Artonne, "Le Recueil des traités de la France composé par ordre de Charles V," in *Recueil de travaux offerts à Clovis Brunel*, 2 vols. (Paris: Société de l'Ecole des Chartes, 1955). I, 53-63. Artonne describes the manuscript as follows: "Le manuscrit est sur parchemin; d'après l'écriture, on peut l'attribuer à la fin du XVe siècle, au règne de Charles VIII ou de Louis XII. La décoration confirme cette attribution; elle se compose essentiellement d'une page enluminée; une bordure renferme une décoration à rinceaux et entrelacs, entremêlés de fleurs des champs et d'animaux; le frontispice comporte les armes de France surmontées par la couronne royale, supportées par deux anges." (54-5)

[7] This text is the companion piece to the text of the *Teachings* published by H. Dusevel in *BSHF*, 10 décembre 1839, 4-7.

[8] Op. cit., Viollet, p. 134.

Chapter II

MEDIEVAL TESTIMONY

There are several late 13th and early 14th century biographers and chroniclers who have left us a life of Saint Louis. Perhaps the best known of these writers is Jean de Joinville, Seneschal of Champagne, who accompanied Saint Louis, and came to know him well, during the six years they spent together in the Holy Land during the Seventh Crusade (1248-1254). Joinville, who wrote his *Histoire de Saint Louis* at the request of Philip the Fair's wife, Jeanne de Navarre (1273-1305), presented the work to their oldest son, the future Louis X, in 1309. Born about 1224, Joinville was already in his eighties when he wrote his *Histoire* and we know that he depended upon one of the many extant manuscripts of the *Grandes Chroniques de France* dealing with the reign of Saint Louis for the text of the Teachings which he included in his work.[1] As for the Instructions, not only does he not include them in his biography of Saint Louis, he does not even allude to their existence.

In 1272, two years after Louis IX's death, Pope Gregory IX asked Geoffroi de Beaulieu, who had been Louis' confessor during the last twenty years of the king's life, to compose a biography of the

---

[1] In paragraph 768 of the Natalis de Wailly edition (1874) of Joinville's *Histoire de Saint Louis*, the Seneschal of Champagne writes: "Ja faiz savoir à touz que j'ai céans mis grant partie des faiz nostre saint roy devant dit, que je ai veu et oy, et grant partie de ses faiz que j'ai trouvés, qui sont en un romant, lesquiex j'ai fait escrire en cest livre. Et ces choses vous ramentoif je, pour ce que cil qui orront ce livre croient fermement en ce que li livres dit que j'ai vraiement veu et oy; et les autres choses qui y sont escriptes ne vous tesmoing que soient vrayes, parce que je ne les ay veues ne oyes."

already semi-legendary Capetian. Geoffroi's *Vita et Sancta Conversatio Piae Memoriae Ludovici quondam Regis Francorum,* [2] completed at some time between this request in 1272 and his own death in 1275, contains a text of the Teachings. Like Joinville's work, however, it lacks both a text of, or any reference to, the Instructions.

Another biographer who left us a life of Saint Louis is Guillaume de Chartres, a friend of Geoffroi de Beaulieu, who accompanied Louis on both of his foreign expeditions. Like Joinville and Beaulieu, Chartres omits from his *De Vita et Actibus Inclytae Recordationis Regis Francorum Ludovici*... [3] both the text, and any mention of, the Instructions. He also, however, fails to include or to mention a text of the Teachings.

Guillaume de Saint-Pathus, a Franciscan, also composed a life of Saint Louis which was most likely originally written in French. [4] Saint-Pathus was the confessor of Queen Marguerite (c. 1221-1295), Saint Louis' widow, during the last eighteen years of her life and then later served as confessor to Louis' daughter Blanche (1253-1323). [5] It was Blanche who initially called upon Saint-Pathus to compose his biography and who saw to it that his work was facilitated by procuring for him a copy of the depositions made during the second of the three canonization inquests conducted prior to Louis' canonization in 1297. With these documents in hand (we are not sure whether Saint-Pathus had at his disposal everything

---

[2] *RHGF*, XX, 3-27. A short biographical note on Beaulieu can be found on p. XXVIII of the same volume. See also: *Histoire Littéraire de la France (HLF)*, XIX (1895), 234-7; and XVI (1875), 133.

[3] *RHGF*, XX, 27-41. Biographical information on Guillaume de Chartres can be found on pp. XXX-XXXIII of the same volume. See also: *HLF*, XIX (1895), 359-62. It is actually quite understandable that Guillaume should omit any reference to the Teachings or Instructions. This is so because his intention in composing his biography was simply to fill in some of the lacunae left by his friend Geoffroi de Beaulieu. This, of course, would explain why Guillaume neglected to include the Teachings in his work. As for his neglect of the Instructions, which are not in Geoffroi's *Vita*, one can perhaps conclude from their absence that Guillaume did not have a text available to him.

[4] Op. cit., Delaborde, *Vie*. Although Delaborde was of the opinion (pp. XI-XII) that the original version of the *Vie* was written in Latin, we disagree with this judgment. The problem is discussed further in Chapter IV of the present study. For further biographical information on Saint-Pathus, see: *RHGF*, XX, pp. XXXIV-XXXVII, and *HLF*, XXV (1898), 154-77.

[5] Delaborde, *Vie*, p. IX.

written down during this inquest or only a part of the total testimony),[6] Guillaume composed his *Vie de Saint Louis* in 1302 or 1303. Probably owing to the fact that of all the biographers of Saint Louis, Guillaume de Saint-Pathus had the largest amount of source material at his disposal, his *Vie* includes not only a text of the Teachings but a text of the Instructions as well.

We have much less biographical information on the other authors who have written on the life of Louis IX. Whereas the above-mentioned writers were essentially biographers, the remaining ones, each of whom was associated with the monastery of Saint-Denis, where the *Grandes Chroniques de France* were written, were all chroniclers and not biographers. The first of the three men we shall treat here is Guillaume de Nangis who composed that part of the *Grandes Chroniques* that covered most of the thirteenth century. In addition to his *Chronicon*, which dealt with the years preceding, including and following the reign of Saint Louis, he also wrote a *Vita Sancti Ludovici*,[7] and both of these works were almost immediately translated into French either by Guillaume himself or by one of his collaborators. In each work, however, he includes a text of the Teachings but fails to include or even to mention the Instructions. Another chronicler at Saint-Denis, a monk named Primat, also composed a *Chronicon*, now lost, dealing with the years of Louis IX's reign.[8] It was later translated into French by Jean du Vignay, a knight of the Hôpital de Saint-Jacques in the

---

[6] Ibid., pp. 3-5. See also: M. Riant, "Déposition de Charles d'Anjou pour la canonisation de Saint Louis," *Notices et Documents publiés pour la Société de l'Histoire de France*, Paris, 1884, pp. 155-76. The canonization process took place, at intervals, for about twenty years. The first inquest dates from 1278-1280, the second from 1282-1283, and the third, culminating in the canonization of Louis IX, from 1294-1297. Also of interest are pp. XV-XVI of *Les Miracles de Saint Louis*, ed. P. B. Fay (Paris: Champion, 1931). Fay, discussing documentation used by Saint-Pathus in composing both the *Vie* and the *Miracles*, believed that there were so many people who made depositions (38 for the *Vie* and 330 for the *Miracles*), that the *copie* that William used was most likely an abbreviated one.

[7] Guillaume de Nangis, *Chronicon*, in *RHGF*, XX, 543-82. *Vita Sancti Ludovici*, in *RHGF*, XX, 309-465. See also: *HLF*, XXV, 118-31. Also of interest are: *Les Grandes Chroniques de France*, ed. Jules Viard (Paris: Klinksieck), VII (1932) and X (1953); *Chronique latine de Guillaume de Nangis de 1113 à 1300*, ed. H. Geraud, 2 vols. (Paris: Renouard, 1843).

[8] *RHGF*, XXIII (1894), 1-5. Primat's *Chronicon* has been lost and survives only in the translation of Jean du Vignay.

early years of the fourteenth century, who wrote at the request of Jeanne de Bourgogne, the wife of Philip VI (1328-1350).[9] Like the works of Nangis, the Primat/du Vignay chronicle includes the text of the Teachings but excludes either a text or any mention of the Instructions to Isabelle.

Finally, there is one monk, a biographer named Yves de Saint-Denis, who does include in his *Gesta Sancti Ludovici Noni Francorum Regis*[10] a mention of the existence of the Instructions. This reference, which shall be described in more detail below, is appended to the text of the Teachings contained in his biography of Louis IX.

As we have already seen, each of these writers (except Guillaume de Chartres) includes in his work a text of the Teachings to Philip. Only one, however, Guillaume de Saint-Pathus, includes a text of the Instructions to Isabelle. Guillaume, who composed his work sometime between December 4, 1302 and October 11, 1303,[11] probably wrote in French and divided his work into two parts. The first, dealing with Louis' life, was presented more in a thematic than chronological order, while the second treated the miracles attributed to Louis' intercession after his death in 1270.[12] Guillaume himself argued for the historical validity of his *Vie* when he wrote in his preface:

> Et en la descripcion des choses que Nostre Sires touz puissanz a deignié fere par le benoiet saint Loys, il m'a semblé que je ne devoie fere force en curieuse et aournée maniere d'escrire, meesmement comme je n'i entende nule chose a metre ne amenuisier, mes ces choses que j'ai veues escrire loiaument si com eles sont escriptes, prouvées et examinées par la cort de Romme et approuvées, pour ce que eles soient crues plus certainement de toute bonne gent.[13]

He then explained to his reader his rationale for the thematic as opposed to a purely chronological recounting of Louis' life:

---

[9] *Chronique de Primat*, in *RHGF*, XXIII, 5-106.
[10] *RHGF*, XX, 45-57.
[11] Op. cit., Delaborde, p. X.
[12] *Les Miracles de Saint Louis*, ed. P. B. Fay (Paris: Champion, 1931). This text also appears in *RHGF*, XX, 121-89.
[13] Op. cit., Delaborde, p. 6.

24 THE INSTRUCTIONS OF SAINT LOUIS

"... je n'ai pas cest oevre toz jors ordie selon l'ordenance du tens pour eschiver confusion, ainçois ai plus estudié a garder ordenance de plus convenable jointure, selon ce que les choses fetes en un meemes tens sembloient estre convenables a diverses matires, ou selon ce que les choses fetes en divers tens sembloient convenir a une meesme matire." [14] Given this thematic bias to Guillaume's *Vie*, we can understand why the Instructions, which were written by Saint Louis near the end of his life, appear in chapter 9 (of 20 chapters) entitled "Ce fine li huitiemes chapitres et commence li noviemes qui est d'amour a ses proismes fervent." [15] In this chapter, which includes complete texts of both the Teachings and Instructions, the Instructions are presented first with the following introduction: "Et premierement il apert que il ait enformé ses enfanz a bonne vie, si com ordre de charité le requiert. De quoi li benoiez sainz Loys envoia a ma dame Isabel, sa fille, roine de Navarre, une letre d'enseignement escrite de sa propre main, de la quele acion la teneur est tele." [16] It is important to note here that despite the fact that Guillaume makes no attempt to date the composition of the Instructions (nor does he make any attempt either at dating the Teachings), he does explicitly state that the Instructions were sent to Isabelle and that they were a "letre d'enseignement."

After furnishing his text of the Instructions, Guillaume appends the following information about other objects and missives sent by Louis to his daughter:

> Li benoiez rois encores envoia a sa dite fille de Navarre deux boistes ou trois d'iviere, et el fons de ces boistes avoit un cloet de fer auquel il avoit liees cheenetes de fer de la longueur d'un coute ou environ; les cheennetes estoient encloses en chascune de ces boistes, des queles la dite royne se disciplinoit et batoit aucune foiz, si com ele recorda a son confesseur quant ele aprocha de la mort. Et encores envoia li diz benoiez rois a cele meesmes fille unes chaiennetes de haire lees ausi comme la paume de la main d'un homme, des queles ele se ceignoit aucune foiz, si com ele recorda a son confesseur el tens devant dit. Et avecques tout ce, li benoiez rois envoia a la dite roine une

---

[14] Ibid., pp. 6-7.
[15] Ibid., p. 58.
[16] Ibid., p. 59.

letre escrite de sa main, en la quele il estoit contenu que il enveoit par frere Jehan de Monz, de l'ordre des Freres meneurs, adonques confesseur de celle roine et aucune foiz du benoiet roy, unes deceplines encloses, si com il est dit desus, et la prioit en cele letre que ele se deciplinast souvent a celes deceplines pour ses propres pechiez et por les pechiez de son chetif pere. [17]

Unfortunately, Guillaume once again offers us no sense of chronology here. Not only is it unclear when the Instructions themselves were composed and sent, we are also left with no concrete dating for the other missives mentioned.

Although none of the other medieval biographers and chroniclers to whom we owe a life of Saint Louis includes a text of the Instructions in his work, two of them mention letters or instructions sent by Louis to his oldest daughter. The first of these biographers is Geoffroi de Beaulieu (Louis' confessor for the last 20 years of his life) who, in the paragraph in which he introduces his text of the Teachings, makes the following comment about a missive sent by Louis to Isabelle:

> Similiter filiae suae primogenitae, quae postea fuit regina Navarrae, cum adhuc esset ipse ultra mare, litteras speciales manu sua transmisit, in quibus inducebat eam efficaciter et devote ad mundi contemptum, et ad religionis amorem et ingressum. [18]

This letter (or letters), personally written by Louis while abroad and sent to Isabelle from there, exhorted her specifically to turn her back on the world and to enter the religious life: "inducebat eam efficaciter et devote ad mundi contemptum, et ad religionis amorem et ingressum." Unfortunately, this description does not coincide at all with the contents of the various texts of the Instructions, for in this latter document, which is addressed to a mature married woman, there is no question of entering religious life. We can only presume therefore that the letter to which Beaulieu refers was written during Louis' first venture "ultra mare" on the Seventh Crusade (1248-1254). Isabelle, born in 1242, would have only been about six to

---

[17] Ibid., p. 63.
[18] *RHGF*, XX, 8.

twelve years old at the time, and it thus would have been more logical for Louis to write to her then in order to exhort her to enter a convent. This letter to which Beaulieu refers has been lost. [19]

The other writer to refer to "instructiones" from Louis to Isabelle is Yves de Saint-Denis. In introducing his text of the Teachings he writes:

> Ea autem quae idem sanctus rex, Deo edocente, per studium vel auditum de scripturae documentis intelligere potuit, alios, praecipue liberos suos, edocere curavit, ut instructiones quas ad Philippum filium suum et ad Ysabellam filiam suam, Navarrae reginam, scripsit, legere ibidem volentibus manifestant. [20]

As we see, Yves does not do much more than mention the "instructiones" written by Louis for his oldest daughter. Although he does not supply his reader with a text of the Instructions, and neglects to tell us anything either of the time and circumstances of their composition or of the way in which they were conveyed to Isabelle, we can safely presume that the text to which he refers is the same one furnished us by Saint-Pathus. Unlike Saint-Pathus and Beaulieu, he makes no mention of an earlier letter (indeed, he does not even state that the Instructions were communicated to

---

[19] Louis Sébastien Le Nain de Tillemont, *Vie de Saint Louis*, 6 vols. (Paris: Renouard, 1847-1851). According to Tillemont (III, 470), Louis was very concerned about the wellbeing of Isabelle after the death of her grandmother in 1252. Since she was now alone and, as Tillemont puts it, "en la garde des hommes," Louis probably felt impelled to write to his ten year old daughter whom he had not seen in four years. It should also be remembered that a child of ten could quite possibly be the recipient of a letter exhorting her to enter a convent — especially when the girl had such a pious father. It is interesting to note that Beaulieu tells us in this regard that Louis had intended that two of his sons, Jehan-Tristan (1250-1270) and Pierre d'Alençon (1251-1284), both of whom were born abroad during the Seventh Crusade, be given over to religious orders (one to the Franciscans and one to the Dominicans) when they reached the age of discretion. He writes: "et inde postquam in Franciam est reversus, ut credimus, spiritu Dei ductus, ordinavit, et in testamento suo scribi voluit, quod duo filii, qui sibi nati fuerant ultra mare, scilicet domnus Jo. et domnus P. cum ad annos discretionis venissent, infra septa religionis nutrirentur; videlicet unus in domo Frat. Praedicatorum Parisius, et alius in domo Fratrum Minorum..." *RHGF*, XX, 7-8. Finally, the best gauge of Isabelle's maturity is the fact that she was only thirteen when her father gave her to Thibaut in 1255.

[20] *RHGF*, XX, 47.

Isabelle in the form of a letter), which, according to Beaulieu, was sent to Isabelle from the Holy Land about the year 1252. We are presuming, therefore, that the "instructiones" to which Yves refers, and the text of the Instructions, are one and the same thing. On the other hand, the second text that interests us here, that is, the earlier one mentioned by Saint-Pathus, may or may not be the one that Beaulieu tells us was sent to Isabelle from "ultra mare." In any case, this other letter (or letters) to which Saint-Pathus and Beaulieu refer, has not survived.

Finally, the relative silence of our medieval sources regarding the Instructions seems to indicate that most of them were unaware of its existence. And even in the one case in which the Instructions are simply alluded to, the very fact that the biographer in question, Yves de Saint-Denis, does not supply a copy of the text whose existence he seems to be affirming, might well indicate that he was unable to procure a copy of it to include in his biography. This point is important, as we shall see below.

It might be mentioned at this point that two of the texts of the Instructions which have survived separately (i.e., not as part of a biography of Louis IX, but simply as short texts included in manuscripts generally devoted to historical matters) do contain a short introduction to the Instructions. These manuscripts, which contain the texts of M and N (both of which were made in the fourteenth century and both of which seem to descend from a common source), state: "Ce sont les enseignemens que le bons roys saint Loys fist et escript de sa main et les envoya de Carthage ou il estoit a la royne de Navarre sa fille." Once again the fact that Louis sent the text of the Instructions, which he had written with his own hand, is confirmed. The statement that they were sent to Isabelle "de Carthage," that is, from Tunis in 1270 while Louis was embarking on the Eighth Crusade, is a fantasy invented by a fourteenth century scribe. The fact is that Isabelle, as Countess of Champagne and Queen of Navarre, accompanied her husband Thibaut on that Crusade and was physically present in North Africa when her father died. For this reason one ought to be cautious in reading the introductory remarks made in these texts.

The last medieval allusion to the existence of the Instructions came in 1374 when Gérard de Montaigu, secretary to King Charles V (1364-1380), discovered a text of the Instructions in the royal

Trésor des Chartes. Before giving this text (which was accompanied by a text of the Teachings) to the king, he had a copy made of it to which he appended the following note:

> L'original de ces enseignemens lequel estoit escript d'une grosse lectre qui n'estoit pas trop bonne, fut trouvé par moy, Gerart de Montagu, secretaire du Roy, ou tresor de ses privileges, chartres et registres dont j'estois garde, et le baillay au Roy en sa tour de Vincennes, l'an mil IIIc LXXIIII, lequel le baitt lors a monseigneur le duc de Bourbon frere la Royne, lesquelz estoient descendus du Roy saint Loys dessusdit et me commanda le Roy que j'en retenisse autant pour garder en son dit tresor. Et aussi pareillement bailla lors le Roy audit duc de Bourbon l'original des enseignemens qui s'ensuivent. [21]

The sense of Montaigu's note is that he believed that the manuscript he had discovered represented the holograph of Saint Louis. Written "d'une grosse lectre," which he took to be the work of Louis IX's untrained hand, the text was apparently accepted by Charles V as the hand-written text of his ancestor, for he in turn passed it on to his own brother-in-law Louis de Bourbon. A copy of this text has survived and can be found in a manuscript currently held in the Bibliothèque Municipale d'Amiens under the title *Traités et Alliances entre la France et les autres Etats*. This manuscript, as its title indicates, is composed of a collection of various royal documents. As such, isolated texts of the Teachings and Instructions are included in it.

In summary, whereas only Guillaume de Saint-Pathus supplies a text of the Instructions, Yves de Saint-Denis, although he does not furnish a text of the document, does mention the existence of the Instructions. As for Geoffroi de Beaulieu, who does not mention the existence of the Instructions, much less furnish a copy of them, he does refer to another letter which Louis sent to Isabelle while he was away in the Holy Land between 1248 and 1254. This letter was probably sent after 1252, i.e., after the death of Blanche de Castille. Guillaume de Saint-Pathus also mentions a second missive, which he does not date and which was delivered to Isabelle by the Franciscan John du Mont. A "deceplines" was enclosed with this undated

---

[21] Op. cit., H. Dusevel, p. 7.

letter and we are not sure if this missive and the one alluded to by Beaulieu are one and the same.[22] None of the other chroniclers and historians alluded to above even mention the existence of the Instructions, let alone include a text of the document in their writings.

---

[22] We treat the question of other letters sent to Isabelle in our Appendix.

Chapter III

CRITICAL CONTROVERSY

The first modern scholar to deal directly with the problems posed by the texts of the Instructions to Isabelle was Paul Viollet. In an article dealing with the subject in 1869, he devoted most of his attention to the textual problems involved in establishing an edition of the Teachings to Philip.[1] But in the five pages of the article which are devoted to an analysis of the texts of the Instructions to Isabelle, he makes the following main point. There are two separate manuscript traditions represented by the various texts of the Instructions, one in a Latinized style of Old French, the other in a purer brand of French uncontaminated by Latinisms. Taking a representative text from each tradition, Viollet argues that of the two different manuscript traditions, the Latinized text, which he attributes to the "confesseur de la reine Marguerite,"[2] owes its contamination to the fact that it was translated from an original Latin text. The other text, the one that is of purely Old French origin, and which he said was not contaminated by Latinisms, presumably did not pass through an intermediate Latin form. Subsequent research by H.-Fr. Delaborde and P. B. Fay has not only identified Queen Marguerite's confessor as Guillaume de Saint-Pathus,[3] but

---

[1] "Note sur le véritable texte des Instructions de Saint Louis à sa fille Isabelle et à son fils Philippe-le-Hardi," *BECh*, XXXV (1869), 129-48.

[2] Ibid., p. 130.

[3] The "confesseur de la reine Marguerite" remained anonymous until H.-Fr. Delaborde established his identity as Guillaume de Saint-Pathus. See: H.-Fr. Delaborde, *Vie de Saint Louis*, pp. VI-IX. See also: P. B. Fay, *Miracles de Saint Louis*, pp. XI-XIV, for comments generally supporting Delaborde's findings regarding the identity of the author of the two works.

has also dated his version of the Instructions and explained his highly Latinized Old French style as follows. If Guillaume did not actually write his own *Vie de Saint Louis* (in which he includes texts of both the Teachings and the Instructions) in Latin, the presence of Latinisms in his work can be explained by the fact that he took as the basis of his biography of Saint Louis the canonization documents put at his disposal by the papal investigators sent from Rome.[4] All these documents, now lost, were in Latin. In any case, this first critical mention of the Instructions to Isabelle by Paul Viollet divides the manuscripts into two separate families or versions, one Latinized and attributable to Queen Marguerite's confessor, and the other free of Latinisms.

Subsequent to Viollet's reference to the Instructions to Isabelle in the above-mentioned article, the texts of the Instructions aroused critical controversy for the most part only in so far as one or another of these texts was accompanied in its manuscript form by one of the various texts of the Teachings to Philip. In other words, the Instructions to Isabelle became a more or less separate critical problem in relation to the Teachings for, once again, thanks to Joinville, the Teachings were much more widely known. But Joinville was not alone in including the Teachings to Philip in his *Histoire de Saint Louis* while excluding the Instructions to Isabelle, for, as we have already seen, all but one of the chroniclers and biographers who wrote a life of Saint Louis in the closing years of the thirteenth century or in the early part of the fourteenth century include in

---

[4] Op. cit., p. 130. Viollet believed that the *Vie* was originally composed in French but that the work subsequently passed through a Latin translation, thereby explaining the Latinisms in it. Delaborde, in *Vie de Saint Louis*, pp. X-XV, argued that the *Vie* was first written in Latin. P. B. Fay, in *Miracles de Saint Louis*, pp. XIX-XXII, agreed with Delaborde on this point. Although, for the purpose of the present study, it is not essential to determine whether the Latinisms contained in the Saint-Pathus version of the Instructions are there because Saint-Pathus wrote in Latin or because he composed his text in French while working from a Latin source, we still believe that he originally composed the *Vie* in French. See: James Westfall Thompson, *The Literacy of the Laity in the Middle Ages* (Berkeley: University of California Press, 1939). In the light of Thompson's study, it is probable that Saint-Pathus, writing for a lady of the court, would compose his work in French, the language of the court. According to Thompson (pp. 144-7), if a lady of the end of the thirteenth century were to be literate, she would be so in French and not in Latin.

their work the Teachings but omit the Instructions. This exception is the above-mentioned Guillaume de Saint-Pathus who, writing at the request of Saint Louis' daughter Blanche de la Cerda [5] and working from information (now lost) gathered at the canonization inquest of 1282-1283, had at his disposal a copy of the Instructions to Isabelle. But the question remains as to why the historians of the monastery of Saint-Denis, who in the thirteenth century were compiling their *Grandes Chroniques de France,* as well as other biographers of the king like Geoffroi de Beaulieu, Guillaume de Chartres, Yves de Saint-Denis, Guillaume de Nangis and Primat/du Vignay all omitted the Isabelle text from the biographies of Louis IX. Could it have been that they considered the Teachings to be more important than the Instructions because Philip was a man, a prince, and an heir to the crown of France whereas Isabelle, although a royal offspring, Queen of Navarre and Countess of Champagne, was still only a woman? Or could it have been because the text was simply not made available to them? We shall return to this point below at the end of Chapter IV and hazard an explanation for this almost universal neglect of the Instructions. (See pp. 48-9.)

In 1912, H.-François Delaborde referred back to the controversy that had taken place more than forty years earlier between Natalis de Wailly and Paul Viollet regarding the texts of the Teachings to Philip. In his two-part article, Delaborde devoted a few words to the Instructions in the midst of his rather lengthy *mémoire* on the texts of the Teachings.[6] His personal conclusion, to put it simply, was that the texts of the Instructions presented no serious critical difficulties. He wrote: "Ainsi que le constatait jadis M. Viollet, le texte des *Enseignements à Isabelle* n'offre pas de difficultés sérieuses et les rapprochements que j'aurai à faire, chemin faisant, avec les Enseignements adressés à son frère, joints à l'édition que je donnerai plus loin, me dispensent d'en faire une étude spéciale."[7] Thus we

---

[5] Blanche (1253-1323), eighth child of Saint Louis, was married to Ferdinand de Castille from 1269 until the latter's death in 1275.

[6] "Le Texte primitif des enseignements de Saint Louis à son fils," *BECh,* LXXIII (1912), 73-100; the *suite* of the article appeared in *BECh,* LXXIII (1912), 237-62.

[7] Ibid., p. 83. See our *Teachings of Saint Louis,* pp. 20-5, for a discussion of the opinions of De Wailly, Viollet and Delaborde with respect to the various texts of the Teachings.

see that Delaborde is apparently in agreement with Viollet's dividing the extant manuscripts into two separate traditions, one Latinized and one free of Latinisms. He also announced here that the relative simplicity of the textual problem presented by the texts of the Instructions was such that the edition of the Instructions that he intended to append to his *mémoire* would suffice as a critical text and exempt him from studying the manuscripts of the Instructions any more closely.

Indeed Delaborde did furnish a text of the Instructions to Isabelle in 1912 but that text raised more questions than it settled. First of all, in establishing his text, Delaborde did not indicate which, if any, of the five medieval manuscripts and four printed texts he was using as his base manuscript. But this basic confusion was compounded by several other omissions. They are:

1. The lack of a critical appraisal of Viollet's separation of the various texts of the Instructions into two separate versions, one Latinized and one free of Latinisms;

2. The absence of any attempt to date or to otherwise describe the manuscripts themselves;

3. The failure to discuss problems relating to the omission, in several of the texts, of certain paragraphs of the Instructions. But in addition to all these omissions, Delaborde proved himself in this article to be so wrongheaded in his interpretation of the critical problems relating to the texts of the Teachings to Philip, that his dismissal of the problem involved in establishing a text of the Instructions ought to be looked at more closely.

In 1928, Charles-Victor Langlois, writing in his four volume monument, *La Vie en France au moyen-âge*,[8] devoted a chapter to the controversy surrounding the texts of the Teachings and Instructions. Unfortunately, he too relegated the text of the Instructions to a minor position in relation to that of the Teachings. In fact, in his estimate, the problems stemming from the texts of the Instructions merited no more than one sentence. He wrote: "Quant aux *Enseignements* à Isabelle, dont il n'existe qu'un texte sans variantes, nous avons suivi, de même, l'édition Delaborde, qui ne laisse rien

---

[8] Charles-Victor Langlois, *La Vie en France au moyen-âge*, 4 vols., (Paris: Champion, 1924-1928). See: Vol. IV (1928), 23-46.

à désirer." [9] This text which left "rien à désirer" was presented in modern French translation by Langlois, primarily because his book was designed to be read by a wide audience of non-specialists. Langlois also seems to have felt, though, that the text of the Instructions, like the text of the Teachings (which was his main concern), had become more or less unrecoverable in its original form because it had passed through a Latin intermediary. Thus when he said that Delaborde's "texte sans variantes" was one that left "rien à désirer," he meant that such was the case because a reconstitution of the original was in his opinion a hopeless task. He seems to have felt that Delaborde, in so far as was possible, had furnished a reasonably good text of the Instructions, but at the same time that text did not reflect, in Langlois' view, the holograph of Saint Louis. Langlois' acceptance of the Delaborde text notwithstanding, we have found several shortcomings in the Delaborde text — shortcomings which we propose to remedy in the present edition.

The last modern scholar to concern himself with the textual problems presented by the Instructions was Léon Levillain, who made his thoughts known in an oral *compte-rendu* delivered to the Société de l'Histoire de France in 1933. [10] Levillain's main preoccupation in his address was to argue on behalf of the importance, in his view, of the text of the Teachings found in the so-called *Noster* manuscript now available in B.N. ms. fr. 12814. [11] His argument, in condensed form, goes like this.

There has long been a problem in discerning what happened to Saint Louis' holograph of the Teachings and Instructions. It is probable that Philip III had them in his possession after his return from North Africa in 1271 and that by the time Louis was canonized in 1297 Philip IV had them in his own personal possession. However, since Philip IV was at loggerheads with the Papacy, he had an important paragraph of the Teachings, the one that calls for the King of France to be subservient to the Pope, [12] eliminated from

---

[9] Ibid., IV, 23.

[10] Léon Levillain, "Discours de M. Léon Levillain, Président de la Société, pendant l'exercise 1932-33," *Annuaire-Bulletin de la Société de l'Histoire de France (ABSHF)*, LXX (1933), 71-84.

[11] We chose this text as the basis for our edition of the Teachings.

[12] Paragraph 27 of the Teachings states: Chiers filz, je t'enseigne que tu soies touz jours devoz a l'Yglise de Romme et a nostre pere l'Apostole, et li portez reverence et honeur si comme tu doiz a ton pere espirituel.

those copies of the Teachings that were to be kept in official archives. Thus, the present day text of the Teachings found in Registre AA4 of the Bibliothèque Municipale d'Amiens, which register was a part of the Trésor des Chartes at the end of the thirteenth century, omits this article on the Pope. It was thought by Philip, says Levillain, that to place an altered form of the Teachings in a royal archive alongside an unaltered text of the Instructions (which, containing no article on the Pope, presumably required no political emendation) was to gain credibility for this altered text of the Teachings. Levillain also points out in support of his theory that Philip IV was known to have had other historical texts altered when they were placed in the royal archives in order that the official historical record would always support his viewpoint.[13] For this reason, says Levillain, Philip most likely placed the holographs of the two texts in the Chambre des Comptes for they still seemed to be there some thirty years later under the reign of Philip VI (1328-1350). Meanwhile, he contends, the falsified copy of the Teachings and the authentic, integral copy of the Instructions remained in the Trésor des Chartes and are still available to us in Registre AA4. Now since the above-mentioned holographs were destroyed in the fire that demolished the Chambre des Comptes in 1737, we must look elsewhere if we seek to reconstitute Saint Louis' original texts. They are to be found, says Levillain, in the following places. A copy of the holograph of the Teachings exists in the so-called *Noster* manuscript,[14] because this text was copied from the one originally deposited in the Chambre des Comptes but later destroyed in 1737. As for a copy of the holograph of the Instructions, it is to be found in AA4 because, says Levillain, it resembles so closely the text of the Teachings found in the *Noster* manuscript: "la similitude de ce texte [AA4] avec celui des Enseignements à Philippe dans le registre *Noster*, dans leurs parties communes, nous oblige à considerer celui-ci comme une copie de l'original."[15] Levillain also declares, however, that when he compared the texts of the Teachings and Instructions found in AA4 with those contained in B.N. ms. fr. 25462, he discovered that "ces copies de 1374 sont, à quelques variantes près, identiques à celles du manuscrit [25462]

---

[13] Ibid., Levillain, p. 82.
[14] See our *Teachings*, pp. 40-5.
[15] Ibid., Levillain, p. 84.

du fonds français de la Bibliothèque nationale." [16] Furthermore, says Levillain, the texts of the Teachings and Instructions found in 25462 once belonged to the Trésor des Chartes: "Dans le manuscrit 25462 du fonds français de la Bibliothèque nationale dont l'écriture est de la fin du XIIIe siècle ou des premières années du XIVe, on trouve les deux Enseignements; le copiste atteste qu'il les a tirés du Trésor des Chartes." [17] Unfortunately, Levillain did not push his analysis of the relative merits of AA4 and B.N. ms. fr. 25462 any further than this.

Finally, our last reference to the critical controversy surrounding the texts of the Instructions to Isabelle has to do with that text of the Instructions appended by Claude Ménard to his 1617 edition of Joinville's *Histoire de Saint Louis*. [18] This text is of interest especially because the editors of the *Recueil des Historiens des Gaules et de la France* claimed that it was based on a manuscript that once belonged to the Chambre des Comptes. [19] Thus, if Levillain's assumptions about the holographs of the Teachings and Instructions until the fire of 1737 are true, that is, that they were stored in the Chambre des Comptes until they were ravaged by fire in that year, then this copy made in 1617 from a text on deposit in the Chambre des Comptes is of potentially great value. This text will be examined below, as will the contention that it once belonged to the Chambre des Comptes.

---

[16] Ibid., p. 82.
[17] Ibid., p. 81.
[18] Jean de Joinville, *Histoire de Saint Louis*, ed. Claude Ménard (Paris: 1617), pp. 356-9.
[19] *RHGF*, XX, 302. Delaborde, in his article cited above (*BECh*, LXXIII (1912), 82), comments on this claim. He supports our view expressed below on p. 46. He agrees that Ménard does not state that the text he found had once belonged to the Chambre des Comptes. See Chapter IV, note 4.

Chapter IV

TEXTUAL ANALYSIS

The evidence adduced from medieval sources with regard to the Instructions, when coupled with the various viewpoints emitted in the course of the subsequent critical controversy, has not led to the establishment of a definitive critical text of the Instructions. As noted above, it seems certain, based on medieval testimony, that the Instructions were hand-written by Saint Louis toward the end of his life and that they were sent to Isabelle. Also, from among all of Louis' biographers, only one, Guillaume de Saint-Pathus, has given us a text of the Instructions. Meanwhile, one other writer, Yves de Saint-Denis, refers to the existence of the Instructions but does not furnish a text of the document. The Saint-Pathus version of the Instructions (we recall that there are four extant texts of this version) was composed with the official canonization documents as its point of departure. This fact vouches for the historicity of the Instructions found in Saint-Pathus' *Vie*, but it does not necessarily testify for their literal accuracy since the source documents were themselves written in Latin. For this reason, the Saint-Pathus version of the Instructions can represent the holograph of Saint Louis only indirectly. If, for the sake of argument, we presume that Saint-Pathus originally wrote in Latin, the text of the Instructions that he would have included in his biography of the king would have been a Latin translation of Louis' holograph. But if we assume that he wrote in French (and this is indeed our assumption),[1] we must recall that Saint Pathus' source was a Latin

---

[1] See Chapter II, note 4 and Chapter III, note 4.

one and for this reason the text of the Instructions which he included in his *Vie* is itself the translation back into French of the holograph which had originally been translated into Latin by the Roman canonization investigators. For this reason we should not be too surprised if we find that the Saint-Pathus version of the Instructions is tainted with Latinisms.

As mentioned above, the first modern critic to write of the Latinisms to be found in the Saint-Pathus version of the Instructions was Paul Viollet. Writing in 1869, Viollet noted several syntactic differences between the Saint-Pathus version of the Instructions and those texts of what he referred to as the purely French version of the Instructions, but he did not attempt to offer a critical text. H.-Fr. Delaborde finally did attempt a critical text in 1912, but, as noted above (pp. 32-33), the text remains inadequate. We therefore propose to examine each of the texts of the Instructions in order to determine if a systematically established critical edition is feasible and, if so, to establish it.

Our first task in this matter is to determine the relative merits of the various texts of the Saint-Pathus version. Henceforth, when we refer to the Saint-Pathus version we shall have in mind the text of the Instructions found in his *Vie* (ed. Delaborde) and based on B.N. ms. fr. 4976. It is our opinion that the Saint-Pathus version is indeed Latinized whereas none of the other texts of the Instructions has ever passed through a Latin stage. But this relative reliability cannot be solidly established until it is clearly shown that these other texts escaped the Latinizing tradition to which the Saint-Pathus version was subjected. Since the Roman canonization documents on which Saint-Pathus purportedly based his text of the Instructions are lost, and since no other Latin text of the Instructions is known to exist, we cannot demonstrate the Latin influence in the Saint-Pathus version by comparing it to a Latin text from which it might have been derived. This renders our task somewhat more difficult and also dictates, to begin with, a comparative approach between the Saint-Pathus version (E) and a representative (G) of the purportedly non-Latinized texts.

In employing this method, the first unequivocal Latinism to be found in the vocabulary of the Saint-Pathus version appears in paragraph five:

TEXTUAL ANALYSIS

SAINT-PATHUS   Je vodroie que vous seussiez bien penser as œuvres que li benoiez Filz Dieu a fet pour nostre redemption.

B.N. ms. fr. 25462   Je vaurroi ke vous seussies bien penser as œvres ke li benois Fius Diu fist pour nostre raenchon.

Putting aside the peculiarities of spelling in *picard* dialect, i.e., *ke* for *que* and *raenchon* for *raençon,* let us focus our attention on the form of the last word in each sentence. All of our texts use the word *raençon* (M - *rençon,* N - *raençon,* K - *raençon*) except the texts of the Saint-Pathus version which employ a learned word, *redemption,* presumably indicative of the Latin intermediary *redemptionem.*

Another example of this Latin influence can be found in paragraph twelve. Once again, the respective texts read as follows:

SAINT-PATHUS   Se vous avez aucune tribulacion de cuer, se ele est tele que vos la puissiez et doiez dire a vostre confesseur, dites li...

B.N. ms. fr. 25462   Se vous aves aucune malaise de cuer... dites le a vostre confesseur...

The word which we take to be a Latinism here is *tribulacion,* which is rendered in all the texts of the non-Latinized version by the word *malaise* (G) or *mesaise* (KMN). It is our belief that Saint Louis originally wrote *mesaise* (*malaise*) and that *tribulacion* was derived by Saint-Pathus from the word *tribulationem* which he found in his Latin source.

In paragraph eight we find another expression which surely indicates a Latin influence in the Saint-Pathus version. Before analyzing this Latinism, however, it ought to be recalled that the Instructions and the Teachings have many paragraphs in common and often agree with each other word for word. In our edition of the Teachings we divided that work into thirty-two paragraphs, while the Instructions can be divided most conveniently into twenty-two paragraphs. In each case, the paragraphs that match each other to varying degrees are:

TEACHINGS	INSTRUCTIONS
1	1
2	2
3	3
4	6
5	10
6	11
7	7
8	8
9	13
10	12
11	9
15	17
20	14
31	20
32	22

As stated above, we have no Latin text of the Instructions. We do, however, have Yves de Saint-Denis' Latin text of the Teachings, and this text can be of use to us in identifying Latinisms in the Saint-Pathus version in those cases where the Teachings and the Instructions treat the same subject using similar, and in some cases, identical language. Thus, in paragraph eight of the Teachings, we can use this Latin text of the Teachings to help demonstrate the Latin influence in the Saint-Pathus version of the Instructions. Here, firstly, are the pertinent texts of the Instructions:

SAINT-PATHUS   Dites voz eroisons en pes par bouche et par pensee et especiaument quant li cors Jhesu Criz sera presenz a la messe; et par espace de tens avant, soiez plus en pes et plus entendible a oroison.

B.N. ms. fr. 25462   Vos orisons dites en pais ou par bouche ou par pensee, et, especiaument entrués con li cors Nostre Signour Jhesu Cris sera presens a la messe, soiiés plus en pais et plus ententieve a orison, et une pieche devant.

What interests us in particular here is the following phrase in Saint-Pathus: *et par espace de tens avant,* rendered in G as *et une pieche devant*. K, although it is a late fifteenth century text, copies its older model faithfully here and agrees: *et une piece devant*; but M and N, which we take to be fourteenth century texts, read *et une piece devant la consecration*. We shall return below (p. 44) to this addition of the words *la consecration* in two of our texts, but for the moment the expression *et une pieche devant* merits further analysis. It is our belief that the expression used by Saint-Pathus, *et par espace de tens avant*, is a Latinism. Despite the fact that we have no concrete Latin text of the Instructions at our disposal to prove in a documentary way that this is so, let us examine paragraph eight of the Teachings which, as stated above, deals with the same subject as paragraph eight of the Instructions. This paragraph in Yves de Saint-Denis' *Vita* reads as follows:

> dic in pace orationes tuas vel ore vel mente, et specialiter sis magis in pace et magis intentus, quandiu corpus Domini nostri Jesu Christi praesens erit in Missa, et per spatium temporis ante.

Now the expression *et per spatium temporis ante* in our view represents the Latin expression that Guillaume de Saint-Pathus is translating with the words *et par espace de tens avant*. The other French texts, on the contrary, are free of this Latin influence.

We have another example, this one much more purely syntactical and somewhat less idiomatic, of this same Latin influence in the first sentence of the same paragraph eight. Here are the two texts:

SAINT-PATHUS	Chiere fille, oiez volentiers le service de sainte Eglise, et quant vous serez en l'eglise, gardez que vous ne musez pas et que vos ne diez vaines paroles.
B.N. ms. fr. 25462	Chiere fille, oyez volentiers le service de sainte Eglise. Et quant vous seres u moustier, gardes vous de muser et de dire vaines paroles.

When Saint-Pathus writes *gardez que vous ne musez pas* he seems to be using a dependant clause taking the subjunctive because his Latin model did the same. The four texts of the purely French tradition, however, use a perfectly clear and more naturally French infinitive construction: *gardés vous de muser*. The Latin influence becomes much more evident, however, when we compare the two above texts with the corresponding text of the Teachings offered by Yves de Saint-Denis in his paragraph eight:

> Care fili, doceo te quod audias liberter servitium ecclesiae sanctae; et quando eris in ecclesia, cave tibi ne muses, nec vana verba loquaris.

As we see here, the *cave tibi ne muses*, the subjunctive construction which is paralleled in the Saint-Pathus expression *gardez que vous ne musez pas*, has no Latinized equivalent in G. One may therefore conclude that the Saint-Pathus version has undergone a Latin influence.

Perhaps one more example of this influence will suffice to prove that the Saint-Pathus version is indeed Latinized. We shall illustrate our point with a passage from paragraph eleven.

SAINT-PATHUS	Se vos avez aucune prosperité de santé de cors ou autre, regraciez Nostre Seigneur humblement et li sachiez de ce bon gré, et gardez que vous n'empiriez pas de ce par orgueil ne par autre vice; car c'est mout grant pechié de fere guerre a Nostre Seigneur par l'achoison de ses dons.
B.N. ms. fr. 25462	Se vous avez aucune prosperité ou de santé de cors ou d'autre cose, merciiés ent Nostre Signeur humelement et l'en sachiés bon gré; et vous prenés bien garde que de chou n'empiriés ne par orgueil ne par autre mesprison, car chou est mout grans pechiés de guerroiier Nostre Signour pour l'ocoison de ses dons.

There are two different verb forms in the Saint-Pathus version which we take to be indicative of a Latin influence: *regraciez* and *fere guerre*. In each case, the texts of the purely French version give *merciiés* (M - *merciés*, N - *merciez*, K - *merchiés*), and *guerroier* (MNK - *guerroier*). In our opinion, the latter texts are better, more exact and more closely reflect the actual vocabulary of Saint Louis since the words *regraciez* and *fere guerre,* which appear only in the texts of the Saint-Pathus version, seem to have come from Latin antecedents. Furthermore, both verbs seem learned and somewhat stilted and lack the natural, relaxed and conversational way of writing that characterizes both the Teachings and Instructions. Now when we compare this passage to a passage in paragraph six of the Yves de Saint-Denis text of the Teachings, it becomes evident once again that a Latinizing influence is at work in the Saint-Pathus version. Here is the Yves de Saint-Denis text that deals with the same subject:

> Si dominus noster mittat tibi aliquam prosperitatem ut corporis sanitatem vel aliam, tu debes ei regratiari humiliter, et debes cavere tibi, quod ex hoc non pejoreris nec per superbiam, nec per aliud vitium; hoc est enim multum grande peccatum, guerram domino nostro facere ex donis ipsius.

Once again, the close relationship between the Saint-Pathus version of the Instructions and the Latin text of the Teachings given by Yves de Saint-Denis points in the direction of a Latin influence in the texts of the Saint-Pathus version of the Instructions. There is no need to belabor here the close affinity between Guillaume de Saint-Pathus' verbs *regraciez* and *fere guerre* and Yves de Saint-Denis' *regratiari* and *facere guerram.*

Now that we have demonstrated that the Saint-Pathus version of the Instructions is indeed Latinized, and therefore incapable of reproducing for us the holograph of Saint Louis, let us examine more closely the four texts of the uncontaminated French version: B.N. ms. fr. 25462 (G), Amiens AA4 (K), B.N. ms. fr. 22921 (M) and B.N. ms. fr. 916 (N). As we have already seen, M and N are younger texts than G. K, on the other hand, despite the fact that it dates from the late 15th century, seems to have had a good model which it follows closely at times. Since we shall speak of this text at length below, let us concentrate here on M and N which both date from the 14th century and which, as we have demonstrated in two cases already mentioned (see pp. 27-28 and 41), both betray in each of these instances the scribes who copied them. First of all, when the scribes of M and N arbitrarily mention, in introducing the Instructions, that the text was sent by Saint Louis "de Carthage," they are most likely not being historically accurate. Thanks to Guillaume de Saint-Pathus, we know that the Instructions were sent to Isabelle, but Saint-Pathus does not state that they were sent from Tunis (Carthage). The scribes of M and N, or of the common model their two texts derive from, add the words "de Carthage" with the probable intention of clarifying for their 14th century readers Louis' whereabouts at the time they suppose the Instructions were composed. Unfortunately, these scribes were obviously ignorant of the fact that Isabelle had accompanied her husband, Thibaut de Champagne, on this campaign and was therefore in Tunis when her father died there. Likewise, to return to paragraph eight of the Instructions (see pp. 27-28), we can show another instance in which M and N are removed in time from G:

> G   Et especiaument entrués con li cors Nostre Signour Jhesu Cris sera presens a la messe, soiiés plus en pais et plus ententieve a orison et une pieche devant.

> MN   Et especialment tant comme le corps Nostre Seigneur sera present a la messe, soiés plus en paix et plus ententieve a orison une piece devant la consecration.

Not only is the spelling more characteristic of the 14th than the 13th century in these two latter texts, their separation in time, and therefore in spirit, from the composition of Louis' holograph, is demonstrated by the addition of the words "la consecration" at the end of the paragraph. When the scribe who composed G was at work, these two words, which were most likely not written by Louis IX, were not required to communicate the intended sense of the author. But by the time the scribes of M and N copied their texts in the middle of the 14th century, the addition of these last two words was probably deemed necessary to clarify for the reader the sense of the original.

We also have another example in paragraph eight of how the scribes of M and N emended their texts for the benefit of their contemporary 14th century readers. Both G and K use the expression "li cors Nostre Signour Jhesu Cris sera presens a la messe," but M and N reduce the formula (repeated consistently throughout all the 13th century texts of the Teachings and Instructions that we have studied) of adding the words "Jhesu Cris" to "Nostre Signour." Thus, in M and N we see simply "le corps Nostre Seigneur sera present a la messe." The scribes of M and N, or the scribe of the common source they might have worked from, seem to have felt that adding "Jhesu Cris" to "Nostre Seigneur" was a redundancy. For this reason, they simply eliminated these words, just as, inversely, at the end of the same paragraph, they added the words "la consecration" to facilitate the comprehension of their readers. Omissions and additions like these, made in texts written several generations after Louis' death by scribes who were insensitive to the peculiarities of the language used by Louis himself, force us to rule out these texts as base manuscripts for an edition of the Instructions.

We now come to our two remaining texts, G, which dates from around 1300 and which is written in a *picard* dialect, and K, the text found by Gérard de Montaigu in 1374 in the Trésor de Chartes. In deciding which of these two texts is more worthy of selection as a base manuscript, we shall proceed comparatively, checking each text systematically against the text of the Saint-Pathus version since the latter text, although it cannot reflect the holograph of Saint Louis, is nonetheless based on a Latin translation of that holograph. Thus, used cautiously and judiciously, it can be of use in comparing the relative merits of G and K.

The first conclusion we come to in comparing the three texts with each other word for word is that the number of instances in which G and E (printed text of the Latinized Instructions found in Delaborde's edition of Saint-Pathus' *Vie*) agree against K exceeds by far those in which E and K agree against G. A representative sampling of this tendency follows. In paragraph one, for instance, K, in the phrase "salut et amistié de pere," omits the words "amistié de," given by EGMN. In the next paragraph, K omits the phrase, found in the other four texts, "que vous ne feriés de pluisours autres," and offers in its place the phrase "que d'un autre." Likewise in paragraph two it omits in the phrase "enseignemens escris de ma main," the word "escris," given by EGMN. As we see, from the very beginning of the text we get the impression that K is somewhat unreliable since it deletes and changes words and expressions found in all the other texts. In paragraph four the scribe of K carelessly writes "qui a" instead of "a qui" in the phrase

"Ch'est li sires a qui toute creature puet dire." He is in fact so careless here that he writes a phrase that is basically meaningless. We could pursue this comparison in greater detail, but it is hoped that these examples illustrate the inadequacy of K. It cannot be taken as a base manuscript. Reference to the variants appended to our critical text will confirm our assessment of K's unreliability.

Now that we have ruled out E because of the Latinisms contained in the text, decided against M and N because of their removal in time, text and spirit from the holograph of Saint Louis, and put aside K because of its general unreliability, we are left with G. As we have already mentioned, G is written in a *picard* dialect which was surely not the idiom spoken or written by Saint Louis. The text does date, however, from the very end of the 13th or from the early years of the 14th century and it is free of Latinisms. Unfortunately, it is not without certain shortcomings, but the cases in which it seems to contain a faulty reading (that is, where E and K, and sometimes even M and N, agree against it) are few in number. Here is a resumé of such instances.

In paragraph three, in the sentence "Chou est li sires qui envoia son fill en terre et le livra a mort pour nous delivrer de la mort d'infer," we find what at first sight might seem like the following inadequacies in G. It reads *son fill* against *son benoiet fil* (E) and *son cher fil* (K), and *mort d'infer* against *peines d'enfer* (E) and *paine d'enfer* (K). But since M and N support G against E and K in each case (*son filz* and *mort d'enfer*), we cannot say for sure that G is incorrect. For this reason we here retain the reading furnished by G and also do so in the several other cases where M and N support G against E and K.

There are four cases in which we take G to be in error because of relatively minor omissions. In paragraph five, in the phrase "Chiere fille, la mesure dont nous le devons amer, si est amer sans mesure," G omits the direct object pronoun *l* in *si est l'amer sans mesure* given by EKM (N omits the phrase altogether). Although we emend G here to bring it into conformity with the three readings that contradict it, we do not consider this to be a major fault. A second similar case of an omission occurs at the end of paragraph seven. G reads: "Et soiiés de tel maniere par quoi vostre confessours et vostre autre ami vous osent ensignier et reprendre." Against this reading, EKMN agree in adding the adverb *hardiement* after *osent* (*osent hardiement ensignier et reprendre*). We correct G accordingly here. A third example of an omission by G is found at the conclusion of paragraph seventeen. G reads: "Chiere fille, metés grant paine que vous soyés si parfaite que chil qui orront parler de vous..." In opposition to G, EMN read: *si parfaite en tout bien* and M adds *en tous biens*. Once again we correct G here. The fourth case of this kind occurs in the middle of paragraph eighteen. Where G says simply *que vous ne metés*, K reads *me semble qu'il fust bon que vous ne meissiés*, E *m'est avis que ce soit bon que vous ne metez*, and MN *me semble que il est bon que vous ne mettez*. Here, as in the preceding cases, we consider G in need of emendation.

In addition to these examples of rather slight errors of omission on the part of G, we also have three obvious cases where G adds a few words which were most likely not originally contained in Saint Louis' holograph. In paragraph six, in the phrase "que vous vous laisseriés ainchois les membres cauper u detrenchier et la vie tolir," G has added the words *cauper u* lacking in EKMN. Likewise, in paragraph seven, in the phrase "par qui vous soiiés ensignie et doctrinée des choses que vous devés eschiever," the words *et doctrinée* are lacking in EKMN (*ensigniée des choses que*). Finally, at the beginning of paragraph twelve, G reads "Chiere fille, se vous avés aucune malaise de cuer ou d'autre cose," whereas KMN offer *mesaise de coeur* and E *tribulacion de cuer*. We thus changed G to *mesaise de cuer* because of what seems like a faulty reading.

There are two remaining points, each of great importance, to be made about the text of G. First, there is contained in G what might seem at first glance to be a major flaw: it omits all of paragraph fifteen. Upon closer examination, however, we discover that this omission is most likely due to a scribe's error in copying his model. Since there does not seem to be any conceivable extra-textual (i.e, political or perhaps religious) reason why anyone would want to eliminate the paragraph, it is probable that a copying error resulted from the scribe's confusion or carelessness in beginning paragraph sixteen. [2] Since paragraph fourteen ends with the word *povreté*

---

[2] We raise the question of a deliberate omission because, as we recall, Philip IV is known to have had the texts of the Teachings tampered with. Also, KMN omit paragraph twenty-one of the Instructions and this omission, discussed in detail below, does seem to have taken place for what we can call extra-textual reasons.

and fifteen is terminated with the word *renommee*, perhaps these words with similar endings contributed to his temporary lapse in fidelity to his model. It is doubtless a serious omission, but at the same time it is not an altogether incomprehensible one. When weighing this omission, and the explanation we offer for it, against the general faithfulness and dependability of G (in this regard it is worth noting that G remains completely faithful to the two-case declension system), we think that G still merits being seriously considered as a candidate for base manuscript. The second point to be made about this text is one that argues strongly on behalf of its authenticity. Near the end of the Instructions, the semi-official Saint-Pathus text (E) contains a paragraph that is omitted by all the other texts except G, which includes most of it. This paragraph, number twenty-one, reads as follows:

SAINT-PATHUS   Je vous commant que nul ne voie cest escrit sanz mon congié, excepté vostre frere.

B.N. ms. fr. 25462   Je vous commant que nus ne voie chest escrit sans congiet.

The fact that all the other texts omit the paragraph, whereas G alone agrees with the semi-official E in including it, indicates that G must be based on an early copy of Saint Louis' holograph if not on the holograph itself. The inclusion of this paragraph in G cannot be neglected because it brings us back to one of the essential ideas that Saint Louis communicated to Philip in the Teachings: it incumbed upon Philip, the oldest brother, to assume his father's responsibilities in the event that anything should happen to the latter. This means that Philip knew of the Instructions to Isabelle and was apparently the only person to whom Isabelle could, or did, speak of them. This information is all the more important because Isabelle died in April 1271, only eight months after her father, and when the canonization committee came to France in 1278, it certainly must have been Philip who gave them both the long version of the Teachings and the version of the Instructions which has come down to us in William of Saint-Pathus' *Vie de Saint Louis*. The fact that this paragraph is omitted in KMN can perhaps be explained by reasoning as follows. The scribes who copied the manuscripts surviving to this day all copied manuscripts which had eliminated it because the very act of reproducing this text was in and of itself an act of disobedience against the will of Saint Louis who wanted the existence of the Instructions kept a family secret. Thus, rather than outrightly disobey the wishes of a canonized saint, the scribes in question probably preferred to ignore the existence of this article. In this respect the presence of the article in G is an added proof of the historicity of the manuscript and therefore of its authenticity. Being free of the Latinisms contained in E, it nevertheless goes back to the end of the thirteenth century.

To go one step further, the presence of this paragraph in G and in E helps to explain why the text of the Instructions is so consistently absent from all those chronicles and biographies that do nonetheless record the Teachings. It seems to us that the reason why the Instructions are omitted by writers like Joinville, Beaulieu, Nangis, Primat and Chartres, is that these writers most likely did not have access to a text of the Instructions. And in those instances where they perhaps did see a text of this document, the presence of paragraph twenty-one in it was most likely sufficient to dissuade them from including a copy of the text in their historical works. But if the injunction contained in this paragraph was sufficient to keep chroniclers and biographers from copying into their works a text of the Instructions, it does not seem to us to have been strong enough to have kept these writers from at least mentioning the existence of the Instructions. But since they are also almost universally silent with regard to the very existence of this document, it is our conjecture that they were probably unaware that the text had ever been composed. In other words, Louis' order to keep the Instructions within the narrow circumference of the family seems to have been quite faithfully obeyed, for in addition to Saint-Pathus, only Yves de Saint-Denis refers to a text of "instructiones" which were probably the Instructions to Isabelle. Finally, since the text of the Instructions was never widely circulated in the first place, a text of this document like the one contained in G, that is, one that is faithful to the spirit (and largely to the letter) of the Saint-Pathus text, but without the Latinisms that characterize it and with the inclusion of paragraph twenty-one, becomes all the more important in our attempt to furnish a text that resembles as closely as possible the holograph of Saint Louis.

In conclusion, let us try to relate what we know about these various texts based on our analysis of them, with what the critical controversy surrounding them has established. We recall, first of all, that the editors of the *Recueil des Historiens des Gaules et de la France* reproduced a text of the Instructions which they had found appended to Claude Ménard's 1617 edition of Joinville's *Histoire de Saint Louis*. In introducing this text of the Instructions, they claimed that it had originally been a part of the royal archive known as the Chambre des Comptes: "Claude Ménard a publié (edit. de Joinville, 1617, pp. 356-9), la copie que lui avait communiqué Loisel, de l'*Enseignement de Saint Loys* à son fils, tel qu'il se lisait en des registres de la Chambre des Comptes... Mais Claude Ménard a publié aussi l'*Enseignement de Saint Loys* à sa fille Isabelle; cette pièce est ainsi conçue." [3] But we have examined Ménard's edition of the *Histoire* and nowhere in that work does he state that the text he reproduced had originally been a part of the Chambre des Comptes. On the contrary, in introducing this text he simply states that he is reproducing a text based on a "Manuscrit communiqué par Monsieur Loisel Advocat en Parlement." [4]

But even if this text had at one time belonged to the Chambre des Comptes, it is still not a copy made directly from the holograph of Saint Louis because, like G, it is written in a *picard* dialect which we presume was not the idiom in which Saint Louis composed his

---

[3] *RHGF*, XX, 302.

[4] Jean, sire de Joinville, *Histoire de Saint Loys, IX du nom, roy de France, avec diverses pièces*... ed. Claude Ménard (Paris: 1617). The Teachings are presented by Ménard on pp. 351-6 and the Instructions on pp. 356-9. By way of introduction to the two texts, Ménard writes on p. 351: "Nous serons excusez si pour la conservation de l'antiquité, et mesmes authorisation de cette instruction, nous en employons une autre differente en quelque chose, qui montrera le langage de ce temps-là, qui a esté tiree d'un Manuscrit, communiqué par Monsieur Loisel Advocat en Parlement, assez recogneu par son nom et ses escrits." Then on page 356, in introducing the Instructions, he writes: "Il en feist autant à Madame Ysabeau Royne de Navarre sa fille, que nous insererons pareillement en ce lieu, pour servir de depost à si riches pièces, derniers chants de ce Cigne divin." One last oddity about this book is that pages 353 and 354 are missing. The text of the Teachings contained here is complete and uninterrupted, but in numbering the pages the editor made a mistake in posting numbers at the top of the pages. Thus the Teachings are found on pp. 351-6, but in reality this is only a four page text because two pages (pp. 353-4) are missing. See Chapter III, note 19.

original. Now not only does this Claude Ménard text (H) share a dialectical similarity to G, it also resembles this latter text so closely when it is compared to it, that one is led to state that if the Ménard text is not a copy of the text found in G, the two texts are at least quite closely related and most likely depend upon a common source. In summary, despite the erroneous claim of the editors of the *RHGF* that the text appended by Ménard to Joinville's *Histoire* was once a part of the Chambre des Comptes (and therefore potentially a document that could have been filed there by a royal successor to Saint Louis), this text does not in fact take us any closer to the holograph of Saint Louis than does G.

Finally, as we noted above in comparing G with K, the scribe of the latter text is often careless and this resultant lack of dependability in K militates, by and of itself, against our taking it as a base manuscript. But what of Levillain's claim (see above pp. 34-36) that K, as a text that was probably placed in the Trésor des Chartes by Philip the Fair, is an *integral* copy of the text of the Instructions that Philip had had made in the hope that its presence together with an *altered* text of the Teachings to Philip III would gain credence for this document? As we see this problem, it is difficult to either accept or reject Levillain's argument because the principal proof he adduces for this tampering on the part of Philip IV with the text of his grandfather's Teachings is that since Philip is known to have tampered with other documents he probably did the same with this one. If, however, one accepts Levillain's conjecture, that is, that Philip had the text of the Teachings emended so as to delete the paragraph calling upon Philip III to be subservient to the Pope, one ought to push his conjecture to its logical conclusion. This conclusion, it seems to us, would be that if one agrees that Philip IV did have a paragraph stricken from the text of the Teachings for political reasons, he might also very well have ordered that paragraph twenty-one of the Instructions, the one in which Isabelle is ordered to show the Instructions to no one, be deleted from the text of the Instructions. This would explain the absence of this paragraph in the text of the Instructions found in K. Unfortunately, Levillain seems to have been unaware of this deletion in K, for if he had been aware of it he might not have tried to present K as a copy of Saint Louis' holograph. Our own analysis of this text has adequately demonstrated that even if it were a copy of Louis' holograph (and it most assuredly is not), it would have to be considered as a very poor one indeed.

If, on the other hand, we reject Levillain's contention that the Registre AA4 was originally intended, as a part of the Trésor des Chartes, to contain an integral copy of the Instructions in the hope that it would help lend credence to a falsified copy of the Teachings, we are not doing so in the face of any compelling evidence. In fact, the evidence we have presented thus far indicates not that the text of the Instructions in K is integral but that, if anything, it is both unreliable and fragmentary in so far as it eliminates an important paragraph. We thus remain skeptical about Levillain's contention that the texts of the Teachings and Instructions found in Registre AA4 (K) were originally placed in the Trésor des Chartes by Philip IV for any reason whatsoever.

With regard to Levillain's second basic claim, that is, that the texts of the Teachings and Instructions found in AA4 and B. N. ms. fr. 25462 respectively bear a strong resemblance to each other, we are also somewhat skeptical. We do concede that upon a hasty and superficial reading of the two texts, one could say with Levillain that "ces copies [of the Teachings and Instructions] de 1374 sont, à quelques variantes près, identiques à celles du manuscrit du fonds français de la Bibliothèque nationale [25462]."[5] But when one subjects the two texts of the Instructions to close scrutiny, as we did in Chapter IV, one discovers that the word "identiques" is hardly an appropriate term. Not only is G much older than K, there are also many textual differences between the two — not to mention the fact that they are also written in different dialects, K in *françien* and G in *picard*.[6]

As for Levillain's third major contention, namely that manuscript B.N. ms. fr. 25462 (G) once belonged to the Trésor des Chartes and thus could have, like Registre AA4 (K), been put there by Philip IV, we remain profoundly skeptical. When, speaking of the texts of the Teachings and Instructions found in B.N. ms. fr. 25462, Levillain states that the scribe of that text "atteste qu'il les a tirés du trésor des Chartes," we cannot agree with him for the simple

---

[5] Op. cit., Levillain, p. 82.
[6] Reference to the variants appended below will illustrate that this text (K) is quite unreliable in comparison to G.

reason that we have examined this manuscript closely and have not been able to find this statement atributed to the scribe by Levillian. [7] This is not to say of course that the texts of the Teachings and Instructions found in this manuscript were never a part of the holdings of the Trésor des Chartes. They might very well have been. But it should be pointed out that the *copiste* does not state that such was ever the case and we also have no other way, at present, of proving that such was ever the case.

Levillain's lack of rigor in dealing with the Instructions can perhaps be explained when we recall that the Teachings to Philip and not the Instructions to Isabelle were his main concern in his address. In addition, the fact that he communicated his ideas in an oral *compte-rendu* and not in a learned article also accounts for his somewhat superficial handling of the textual problems relating to the Instructions.

One last problem remains to be dealt with here, for it ought to be recalled that the semi-official Saint-Pathus texts and G differ in their readings of paragraph twenty-one. They are:

SAINT-PATHUS   Je vous commant que nul ne voie cest escrit sanz mon congié, excepté vostre frere.

B.N. ms. fr. 25462   Je vous commant que nul ne voie chest escrit sans congiet.

In attempting to decide which of these two versions of paragraph twenty-one was most likely written by Saint Louis, let us review the evidence in favor of each one. We recall that the Saint-Pathus text is semi-official in that it is based on the canonization documents of 1282-3. Such cannot be said for B.N. ms. fr. 25462, about which we know comparatively little. From this point of view, the Saint-Pathus reading seems more authoritative than that of G. On the other hand, to argue on behalf of G, let us put ourselves in the place

---

[7] See Henri Omont, *Bibliothèque Nationale, Catalogue Général des Manuscrits Français; Anciens Petits Fonds Français*, 3 vols. (Paris: Leroux, 1897-1902). II, 602-4. The Omont catalogue dates the manuscript from the 13th century. As stated above, we feel that the text of the Instructions contained in this manuscript dates from the very end of the 13th or from the very beginning of the 14th century. In any case, it was written after 1297 since Louis IX is referred to in it as *Sains Loÿs*.

of Philip III when, at some undetermined time after his father's death, he made available to the investigators from the Roman curia the two texts that he had in his possession. Firstly, relations between the French crown and the Papacy had not yet degenerated to the point where Philip III would want to delete that paragraph of the Teachings that calls upon him to be subservient to the Pope as to his "pere espirituel," [8] and indeed there is no such deletion in the Saint-Pathus text of the Teachings. But to give his text of the Instructions to outside investigators against Louis' order that the document be kept in the family might have prompted him to add "excepté vostre frere" to the paragraph to make it clear that he was not violating the wishes of a man who was being considered for canonization. Louis might well have told Philip, when he bestowed the Teachings upon him, that a similar text had been or was about to be composed for Isabelle — and indeed we can think of no reason why he should not have done so. But even if Louis had not told Philip that he was the only other person to know about the existence of the Instructions, it is only logical that this document should nonetheless fall into Philip's hands after the death, in the space of only about eight months, of Louis, Thibaut V and Isabelle. Since Isabelle died as a widow without children, the text of the Instructions which she possessed must have been communicated immediately to Philip since he was her closest surviving relative and because it also seem to have been quite widely known that Louis had written a similar text for him. In a word, since Louis had already told Isabelle in paragraph sixteen to obey "humelement a vostre mari et a vostre pere et a vostre mere es coses qui sunt selonc Dieu," making no mention at all of Philip, and also because the moral prescriptions presented in the Instructions are always formulated in a general and non-specific way, it seems to us that Louis probably did not write "excepté vostre frere" at the end of paragraph twenty-one. It seems to us on the contrary that these words were added by Philip III for the simple and well-intentioned reason mentioned above: he had the text in his possession and in offering it as evidence to support his father's canonization, he did not want to give the impression that he was disobeying his father's wishes.

---

[8] Op. cit., *Teachings of Saint Louis*, p. 59.

TEXTUAL ANALYSIS

In conclusion, despite G's omission of paragraph fifteen, we still consider it to be the best available and generally most dependable text of the Instructions. It dates from the end of the 13th century (or from the early years of the 14th century) and it surely preserves the spirit, if not the letter, of Saint Louis' holograph. Given the fact of G's superiority to all other available texts, we shall take it as our base manuscript in the following critical edition of the Instructions. As for the other texts, their relationship to each other and to G can be conveyed through the following schema.

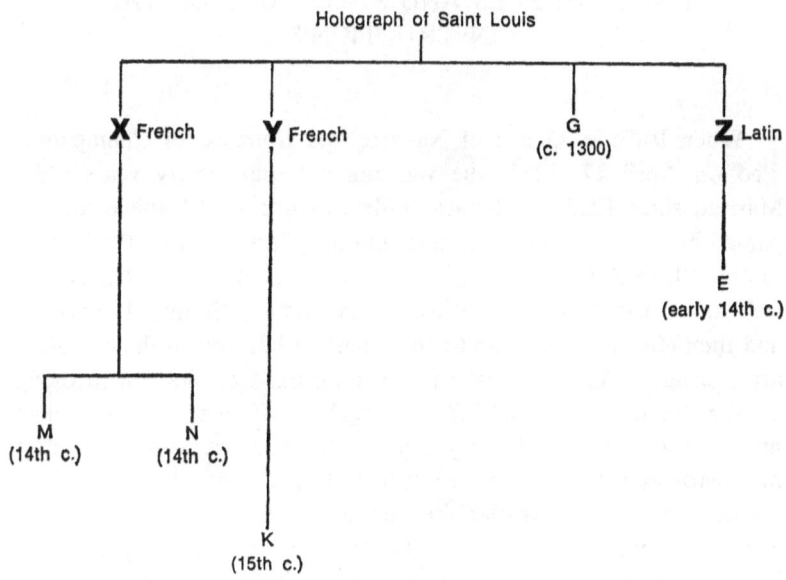

Chapter V

DATE, SOURCES AND STRUCTURE OF THE INSTRUCTIONS

When Isabelle, Queen of Navarre and Countess of Champagne, died on April 27, 1271, she was not yet quite thirty years old.[1] Married since 1255 to Thibaut V de Champagne,[2] Isabelle accompanied her husband on the Eighth and last Crusade in 1270.[3] During the month of August 1270 she witnessed the death of her father as well as of her younger brother Jehan-Tristan, Count of Nevers,[4] and then after the defeat and subsequent withdrawal of the Christian army from North Africa, she lost her husband at Trapani in Sicily on the 4th of December 1270. Allegedly suffering from a broken heart when she passed away herself, Isabelle was described after her death as follows: "In sancta viduitate absque liberis derelicta, sacrae continentiae inviolabiliter servare proponens, luxit maritum et mortem patris fratrisque pia lamentatione quandiu supervixit."[5] Thus, noted for her chaste (and childless) life, Isabelle died far from home and only after she had seen her father, brother and husband precede her to the grave.

Strictly speaking, Isabelle was not the firstborn of Louis IX and Marguerite, for another girl, Blanche (1240-1243), was born before her but died soon after Isabelle's birth.[6] Thus Isabelle be-

---

[1] Le Nain de Tillemont, *La Vie de Saint Louis*, 6 vols. (Paris: Renouard, 1847-51). II, 474. Isabelle's birthday is March 18, 1242.
[2] Tillemont, IV, 59.
[3] Ibid., V, 15.
[4] Ibid., V, 208-9.
[5] Ibid., V, 209.
[6] Ibid., II, 495-6.

DATE, SOURCES AND STRUCTURE OF THE INSTRUCTIONS 57

came the oldest child of Saint Louis only after Blanche's death. Probably named after the mother of Louis VIII, i.e., the grandmother of Saint Louis, Isabelle de Hainaut, Isabelle's youth is largely unknown to us. But by the very fact that she was one of Saint Louis' children, we know that she must have grown up attending mass as well as three or four other religious services each day, and it is also quite possible that her position as oldest child required her to set a special example to the other children.[7] She also must have attended the evening bedtime prayer sessions about which Joinville tells us and during which her father would read or would tell pious exemplary stories to his children.[8] All evidence regarding Louis' raising of his children in which Isabelle is specifically mentioned by name also points in the direction of a pious and devout childhood. We recall, for example, that Geoffroi de Beaulieu tells us of a letter that Louis wrote to Isabelle from the Holy Land, probably around 1252, in which he exhorted her to enter the religious life. Guillaume de Saint-Pathus also tells us that Louis was in the habit of writing to Isabelle to encourage her to cultivate a taste for pious practices and that on one occasion he even sent her a "cheenetes de fer"[9] with which to flagellate herself. Each of these indications, whether of the general background in which she grew up and came to maturity, or of specific references to Isabelle herself, indicates a love of virtue and piety inculcated by an extremely devoted father. This impression is also borne out by the testimony of the chronicler, alluded to by Tillemont, who tells us that when Louis, while in the Holy Land in 1252, found out about the death of his mother Blanche de Castille in Paris, he seems to have been concerned about the safety of Isabelle who, not having accompanied her father in 1248, had remained behind under her grandmother's protection and supervision and who was now left "en la garde des hommes."[10]

When Isabelle was married to young Thibaut V de Champagne in 1255, she was only thirteen years old. The circumstances of the marriage are interesting and one wonders if this daughter, destined

---

[7] Ibid., V, 162.
[8] Ibid., V, 380-3.
[9] *Vie de Saint Louis* by Guillaume de Saint-Pathus (éd. H.-Fr. Delaborde), p. 63.
[10] Tillemont, III, 470.

from childhood for the convent, would have ever been married if a strong request, issued in opportune circumstances, had not been made for her hand. Here is how her marriage was arranged. One of Louis' more pressing and persistent difficulties after his return home in 1254 was in keeping the peace between Hugues le Brun, Comte de la Marche, and Thibaut V de Champagne. While attempting at one point in 1254 to negotiate an end to hostilities between these two powerful vassals, Louis was visited by his close friend Joinville who asked him to give his daughter Isabelle to the Count of Champagne. Louis was willing to do so but only on condition that a permanent peace be established between the two warring parties — and only when all the provisions of the treaty were agreed to by both sides did Isabelle become Countess of Champagne.[11]

In retrospect we can see that Thibaut strongly desired this union with Isabelle. Not only had he broken off an understanding he had reached with the King of Aragon to marry his daughter, he had also worked quietly in other ways to prepare the marriage. Since he and Isabelle were too closely related to marry without a papal dispensation, Thibaut also secured the necessary permission from Pope Innocent IV in November 1254 to allow him to marry Isabelle. Thus, when Thibaut personally pressed his king at a general assembly of all the leading vassals and prelates of the French kingdom to give him Isabelle's hand, he had already nullified the one strong legal reason Louis might have invoked to refuse his request. Once all the details were settled Isabelle and Thibaut were ready to be married, and when they took their conjugal vows at Melun on the 6th of April 1255,[12] Isabelle had just turned thirteen and Thibaut was nineteen years of age.

As King of Navarre and Count of Champagne, Thibaut was obliged to travel quite often between his two disconnected realms in order to fulfill his princely duties in both places. From the time he attained his majority in 1252, thereby taking full possession of his two thrones from his regent/mother, he and Isabelle divided their time between Navarre and Champagne as follows.[13]

---

[11] Jean de Joinville, *Histoire de Saint Louis, Le Crédo et la Lettre à Louis X*, éd. de Wailly (Paris: Le Clere, 1867), p. 447.

[12] Tillemont, IV, 59.

[13] M.-H. d'Arbois de Jubainville, *Histoire des ducs et des comtes de Champagne*, 4 vols. (Paris, 1865). IV, 365-73.

DATE, SOURCES AND STRUCTURE OF THE INSTRUCTIONS 59

Champagne	April 1257	-	April 1258
Navarre	April 1258	-	June 1258
Champagne	June 1258	-	October 1263
Navarre	January 1264	-	December 1264
Champagne	April 1265	-	October 1265
Navarre	November 1265	-	December 1266
Champagne	May 1267	-	February 1269
Navarre	June 1269	-	October 1269
Champagne	November 1269	-	April 1270

The intervals of several months that we have left in this list of Thibaut and Isabelle's travels, indicate in part those times for which we have no definite documentation to prove that they were in either place. For the most part, however, these lacunae represent intervals of travel time required by the royal couple in moving between their two realms.

In our study of Saint Louis' Teachings to Philip, we offered as a tentative date for the composition of that document the period of time between mid-Lent 1267 and Louis' departure from Paris in June 1270.[14] Since Louis convoked all his major vassals and prelates to Paris in mid-Lent 1267 in order to announce his intention to lead another Crusade, and then called all the same people back to Paris again on June 5, 1267 to attend the dubbing of his oldest son and successor, Philip, we took this to indicate an intention on his part to begin making preparations for the ultimate succession of his son to the throne. When, on April 6, 1267, he led a procession outside the walls of the city to the Abbey of Saint-Denis where he publicly resolved to have the remains of all his royal ancestors buried there in one hallowed place, he gave further evidence of this same type of concern. Finally, when he had his last will and testament made out in February 1268, he gave yet another indication that he was very much concerned about the question of continuity and stability in royal affairs after his death.[15] Based on this admittedly circumstantial evidence, we

---

[14] *The Teachings of Saint Louis*, pp. 46-9.

[15] Each of these events is recorded in Tillemont V, 9-121. Louis also did his utmost during this period to arrange for the future well-being of his children. Those who had not already been married off by this time were either scheduled to be married or assured in some other way of an appropriate inheritance.

took April 1267 as our date *a quo* and June 1270 (we presume that the Teachings were not written after Louis' departure from Paris) as our date *ad quem,* and speculated that the Teachings were most likely composed sometime in 1267. In other words, it seemed most likely that they were written before the drafting of the will in February 1268, but after the announcement of the Eighth Crusade, the dubbing of Philip, and the transfer of the remains of the royal ancestors to Saint-Denis in April and June 1267.

The fact that the Teachings and Instructions both contain so many sentences that coincide word for word with each other seems to argue on behalf of a contemporaneous composition of the two texts. In fact, there are several reasons that have led us to just such a conclusion. They are: (1) the resemblance in subject matter between the two texts, (2) the strong resemblance in language and structure of those paragraphs that treat the same subject, despite the fact that the relative order of each paragraph in the whole work is dissimilar in the two texts, and (3) the general tone of the works, for in each one Louis seems to be summing up a lifetime of experience for the future benefit of his two oldest children.

If, as close examination of the many similarities in each text indicates, Louis probably had one text at his elbow, or at least clearly in mind, while he was composing the other, why did he tell Isabelle in the Instructions not to show that text to anyone whereas there is no such *caveat* in the Teachings to Philip? This fact, that is, the presence of paragraph twenty-one in the Instructions, in which Louis tells Isabelle: "Je vous commant que nus ne voie chest escrit sans congiet," does not, in our view, argue against a contemporaneous composition of the two texts. This is so because the Teachings were most likely passed to Philip at a personal, oral interview, whereas the Instructions were probably sent to Isabelle through a messenger. The facility with which Louis could bestow the Teachings upon Philip in a personal interview is self-evident, for the prince, even after his marriage to Isabelle d'Aragon in 1258,[16] resided for the most part in the same household as his father. Isabelle, however, had already been married since 1255, and in her double capacity as Queen of Navarre and Countess of Champagne had to follow the meanderings of her husband's court.

---

[16] Tillemont, IV, 248.

It is probably safe to assume, therefore, that the presence of this paragraph only in the Instructions was necessitated by the fact that Louis and Isabelle usually resided far from each other. When Louis composed the text, the probability of a future visit from his daughter at an early date might have been remote and thus he was perhaps forced to assume, even while writing the text, that it would have to be sent to his daughter and not given to her personally. Wanting to keep secret the Instructions he had taken the trouble to write down for her, he assured that this would be the case by simply stating that such was his wish. Indeed, the presence of this paragraph in the Instructions, given this hypothesis, seems quite logical, and in our opinion only reinforces the probability that the two texts were composed at about the same time. The absence of such a paragraph in the Teachings seems to indicate an interview between father and son at which Louis perhaps told Philip that the Teachings were to be considered as a personal, private communication to be kept between them. But because Isabelle lived apart from her father, he had to stipulate this same intention in writing while he composed the Instructions.

Now when we compare the record of Isabelle's peregrinations with the tentative composition date of 1267-1268, we notice that she was in France and not in Navarre for the period May 1267-February 1268. We know that Thibaut and Isabelle left Navarre on May 5, 1267 [17] and that they visited Paris (where Thibaut agreed to follow his father-in-law on the next Crusade) later on that month. We also known that they returned again to Paris from Champagne in September 1267, but were not to return to Paris again until February 1269. Given these facts, the Instructions were perhaps sent to Isabelle between her May 1267 and September 1267 visits with her father, or between her September 1267 and February 1269 visits with him. In line with our conjecture concerning the date of composition of the Teachings, we would assign the stronger possibility to the period following Isabelle's presence in Paris in May 1267 and preceding Louis' composition of his testament in February 1268. Since Isabelle visited Paris briefly during September 1267, the Instructions were most likely composed between May and September 1267, although they might well have been written between

---

[17] Op. cit., d'Arbois de Jubainville, IV, 365-73.

September 1267 and February 1269. For reasons adduced above concerning the date of composition of the Teachings, it seems that Louis was concerned about problems relating to succession and to the moral well-being of those around him during the period in question. And when his son-in-law, despite the outright disapproval of quite a few other important and trusted men like Joinville, volunteered to accompany him on the Eighth Crusade, Louis could very well have decided that the right time had come to write down a text of Instructions for Isabelle before her departure for the shores of Africa.

* * *

The main source of the Instructions is the very life of Christian action and meditation that Louis had already led before composing his work. The Teachings and Instructions are the culmination of a life-time dedicated to the perfection of Christian virtue and, as such, tell us as much about Louis IX and the century he so splendidly symbolizes, as they do about the practices and attitudes he writes about. For in seeking to convey to Isabelle some notion of what was essentially the conventional moral wisdom of the day, he inevitably gives his reader an insight into his own personal commitment to and interpretation of that wisdom.

Louis IX was an exemplary father. He had all of his children (including his daughters) well educated and saw to it that they could read both in French and in Latin. At night, after assuring that they attended complines with him, he would often read to them and tell them stories taken from the Bible before putting them to bed. [18] These facts are important for if we bear them in mind we see that there is probably nothing in the Instructions that Louis had not already told his daughter orally — either individually or as one of a group of his children — on some previous occasion. In this light, the immediate purpose for which the Instructions were written was perhaps not so much to communicate to Isabelle a few fresh ideas she might never have heard before, but rather to formally codify for her (and perhaps for her descendants as well) those ideas that Louis was anxious to have remembered by posterity. This

---

[18] Tillemont, V, 380-3.

DATE, SOURCES AND STRUCTURE OF THE INSTRUCTIONS 63

document therefore represents a literary act on the part of Saint Louis in that, although it is addressed personally to Isabelle, Louis must have known full well that it would eventually reach a much wider audience. Isabelle is the recipient of the Instructions because of the attachment her father had for her,[19] but by virtue of the fact that Louis took the time to write down and to structure his thoughts, he was quite possibly writing with this potentially larger audience in mind. Indeed, is it not logically consistent that a king so conscious of the value of didactic writing, and so dedicated to the copying and collecting of books, try his own hand at writing? After all, had he not assembled a great royal library at Paris and was not his capital the city that contemporaries of all nations considered to be the successor to Athens and to Rome? And if, as the *Grandes Chroniques de France* tell us, the coming of the Christian religion to France was symbolized in the person of Saint Denis the Areopagite, and if the transfer of chivalrous tradition from the Roman Empire to France was symbolized by Charlemagne, France still lacked a symbol for what contemporaries took to be the great virtue of thirteenth century civilization as it existed in Paris. For when the chroniclers talk of "sens" being the great virtue that Paris had added to "foi" and "chevalerie," they perhaps had in mind the resident intellectuals, the university and the collective wisdom it had gathered together in its theology faculty — and it is this wisdom, this "sapience," that Louis is trying to communicate to Isabelle in the Instructions: the wisdom, the "sens," the "sapience" of a life based on faith in Jesus Christ.

> Quar puis que Nostre Seigneur Jhesu Criz vout especiaument, sus touz autres roiaumes, le roiaume de France enluminer de foi, de sapience et de chevalerie, les rois de France acoustumerent a porter la fleur de lis painte par III fueilles ausi comme s'il deissent par tout le monde, foi, sapience et chevalerie sont par la provision et par la grâce de Dieu plus habundanment en nostre roiaume que en ces autres. Les II fueilles de la fleur de liz qui sont œles (ailes) senefient senz et chevalerie et deffendent la tierce fueille qui est en milieu d'elles, plus longue et plus haute, par laquele est senefiée foi. Car foi est et doit estre

---

[19] Ibid., V, 382. Along with Jehan-Tristan, Isabelle was Louis' favorite child.

> gouvernée par sapience et deffendue par chevalerie. Tant comme ces III grâces de Dieu seront forment et ordenéement jointes ensamble ou roiaume de France, le roiaume sera fort et ferme. Et se il avient que elles en soient ostées ou dessevrées, li roiaumes cherra en desolacion et en destruction. [20]

As stated above, Louis IX had two favorites among his many children: Isabelle and Jehan-Tristan. This latter child was the first one born to Louis and Marguerite overseas (1250), [21] and was to die a few weeks before his father at Tunis in 1270. [22] Despite this alleged preference that Louis had for young John, no set of moral instructions of any kind is known to have been addressed to him. Teachings, however, were written for Philip since he was Louis' oldest son and successor and the Instructions were written for Isabelle in part perhaps because she was the oldest child in the family but mainly, one suspects, because his father was especially attached to her. Strictly speaking, of course, Isabelle was not the oldest child of Saint Louis in the sense that she was not the first born of all the children. Another girl, Blanche (1240-1243), had been born before her. [23] This Blanche, who died in early childhood, was presumably named after Saint Louis' mother, Blanche de Castille, just as the third child born to Louis and Marguerite, Louis (1244-1260), [24] was named after Louis VIII. We also presume that just as the first and third children of the family were named after Louis IX's parents, the second and fourth children, which is what Philip and Isabelle were respectively, were named after Saint Louis' grandparents, Isabelle de Hainaut and Philippe-Auguste. Thus when Louis embarked for the Holy Land in 1248, he left these two children behind in the care of their grandmother — and this lengthy absence from them during the next six years perhaps served to

---

[20] *Grandes Chroniques de France* (éd. Jules Viard), 10 vols. (Paris: Klincksieck), X (1953), 11-12.

[21] Tillemont, III, 335.

[22] Ibid., V, 162. See also: Larry S. Crist, "The Legendary Crucifixion of Jehan Tristan, Son of Saint Louis," *Romania*, LXXXVI (1965), 289-306; and Alfred Foulet, "Jehan Tristan, Son of Saint Louis, in History and Legend," *Romance Philology*, XII:3 (February 1959), 235-40.

[23] Ibid., II, 495-6.

[24] Ibid., IV, 215-6.

DATE, SOURCES AND STRUCTURE OF THE INSTRUCTIONS 65

endear him to them both, but especially to Isabelle, after his return in 1254.[25]

Given this special bond of affection between Louis IX and his daughter as well as his custom of consistently bestowing moral advice on all of his children, we can now examine some of the places where Louis might have been influenced by contemporaries. Of immediate interest in this regard are the *Specula Regis* that were addressed to Louis or to members of the royal family during his lifetime. Two such works were composed by the great *encyclopédiste* of the thirteenth century, Vincent de Beauvais. Although Vincent was not himself the tutor of the royal children (this function was exercised by a *clerc* named Simon), he does seem to have had a theoretical responsibility of some kind for Louis' children's upbringing. His *De Eruditione Filiorum Nobilium*,[26] written between 1247 and 1249 at the request of Louis' wife, Marguerite, was probably intended to guide Simon in the instruction of Isabelle and Louis (1244-1260), while his other work, addressed directly to Saint Louis and composed between 1260 and 1263, is a *floriligium* that quotes many ancient and medieval sources on the principles that were generally accepted at the time as being the rudiments upon which to base the education of a prince. This work, entitled *De Morali Principis Institutione*, is more theoretical and less immediately practical than the *De Eruditione*. The use to which Vincent thinks Louis should put this work is indeed worth noting, for Louis probably had a similar didactic purpose in mind when he composed his own two texts:

> To the most famous and most religious men and illustrious lords and princes worthy of all honor and reverence

---

[25] One can only guess at the influence that Louis' sister, Isabelle de France, could have either exerted on Isabelle herself or on Louis' notion of what young Isabelle should become as an adult.

An ascetic, pious person by nature, Isabelle de France steadfastly refused to allow herself to be married and eventually withdrew to a convent to spend most of her life in isolation. Could Louis have wanted his daughter to grow up like her aunt? We cannot say. See Elie Berger, *Histoire de Blanche de Castille* (Paris: Thorin, 1895), pp. 324-5. According to Berger, a *Vie d'Isabelle de France* by Agnès d'Harcourt was published "par Du Cange, à la suite de son édition de Joinville, 1668" (p. 169).

[26] Vincent of Beauvais, *De Eruditione Filiorum Nobilium*, ed. Arpad Steiner (Cambridge, Mass.: Mediaeval Academy of America, 1938).

in Christ, to Louis, by the grace of God King of the French, and to Theobald, by the same favoring clemency King of Navarre and Count of Champagne, brother Vincent of Beauvais of the Order of Preachers, salutation in the Saviour of all men.

Formerly, while I was staying in the monastery of Royaumont in order to exercise the office of lector according to the will of your Sublimity, O Lord my King, I noticed there that you and your family paid diligent attention with both ears and mind during the sermons; therefore it seemed useful to me to collect something, succinctly divided up into distinct chapters, from the many books which I had read at one time pertaining to the morals of princes and courtiers so that I and the other brethren might have something special in readiness concerning this matter about which truly little is found written, to which we could have recourse opportunely, if by chance it should fall upon us to instruct either privately or publicly these kinds of men concerning the conduct of life and the salvation of their souls as befits the state of each one; namely, princes, soldiers, counsellors, ministers, bailiffs, provosts, and others, either residing at court, or outside it, who administer the common weal. [27]

This point is important for it is symptomatic of the age. As Vincent admits, there is really nothing new or original in his treatise. On the contrary, every idea in it has been tested by time and its validity attested to by authority. For this reason, if Louis ever needs a reminder or would like a written record of all this accumulated wisdom, he will find it here written down for him and for posterity. Vincent's frank and straightforward statement about his sources and about the purposes of his work also applies, in our view, to Louis IX's point of view in composing the Instructions. The document was meant to live longer than its composer and to serve as a reminder and as a source of inspiration at a time when

---

[27] Astrik L. Gabriel, *The Educational Ideas of Vincent of Beauvais* (Notre Dame, Indiana: The Mediaeval Institute, 1956), pp. 43-4. We offer this citation in English because we have been unable to obtain a copy of the Latin text. According to Gabriel, the only extant printed edition dates from the 15th century: Rostochii, Fratres domus horti viridis, ca. 1476. He also mentions the existence (p. 43) of three mss. of the *De Morali,* each of which is currently held on microfilm at the Mediaeval Institute of the University of Notre Dame.

he would no longer be present. Thus, although we can safely say that Louis was aware of the existence of both the *De Eruditione Filiorum Nobilium* and the *De Morali Principis Institutione*, we cannot say that either work exercised a direct influence over Louis while he was composing the Instructions. These treatises, despite their belonging to the same ancient tradition as the one to which the Instructions belong, most likely bore no direct influence on Louis' own writings and thus for our purposes are perhaps best considered simply as works that mirror Louis' concern with establishing and codifying a set of rules destined to insure a happy and balanced Christian way of life.

Another contemporary work that we know to have been written for and dedicated to Saint Louis was Guibert de Tournai's *Eruditio Regum et Principum*. Completed and presented to the king in October 1259, [28] Guibert's treatise proposed as its goal the instruction of the king and of those around him: *et in rege multitudo principum informetur.* [29] Since the work deals mainly with questions of a political nature and also seems to owe much to the work done by Vincent de Beauvais along parallel lines, [30] we think it most appropriate to simply indicate the existence of this text without beginning to speculate about the degree to which it might have influenced Louis. Kervyn de Lettenhove, writing about this very problem, summed it up as follows: "s'il est impossible de déterminer dans des questions spéciales et isolées l'influence que Guibert de Tournay put exercer sur Louis IX, on peut affirmer qu'elle ne fut pas sans quelque fruit, puisque le roi réclamait ses conseils." [31]

The same must be said of the other treatises we know to have been written for and dedicated to Louis or to members of his immediate family. This includes the *Liber Tertius De Informatione Regiae Prolis Ad Margaritem Illustrem Reginam Francorum*, written

---

[28] Guibert de Tournai, *Eruditio Regum et Principum*, éd. A. de Poorter (Louvain: Institut Supérieur de Philosophie, 1914).

[29] Ibid., p. 9.

[30] According to de Poorter, Tournai leans heavily on Vincent de Beauvais' *Speculum Doctrinale*: "C'est là, au livre huit, *De Scientia Politica*, que Guibert a pris le cadre et certaines indications pour son travail" (p. 10).

[31] Kervyn de Lettenhove, "Conseils sur les devoirs des rois, adressés à saint Louis par Guibert de Tournay," *Académie Royale des Sciences, des Lettres et des Beaux-Arts de Belgique. Brussels. Commission Royale. Bulletins.* 1ière série, XX (1853), 496-505, p. 497.

by the Italian Dominican Bartholomäus Vincentinus [32] for Queen Marguerite around 1260, and the *Morale Somnium Pharaonis Sive De Regis Disciplina* written by the Cistercian Jean de Limoges [33] around 1255 or 1260 for the edification of Louis' son-in-law, Thibaut. Each of these works covers, in varying degrees, a part of the subject matter treated by Louis in the Instructions. But since all these texts were written in an age when the wisest teachings and counsels were those that were based on traditional and authoritative sources, it seems to us an idle exercise to attempt to discover where Louis might have found a given idea or turn of phrase. His written work belongs to an ancient line of moralistic endeavor and for this reason it is best understood as a part of that tradition — a tradition in which many men, each in his own way, often did nothing more than reformulate conventional wisdom.

* * *

One of the most concrete images of Saint Louis to be communicated to generations of French school children is the celebrated exchange, recorded by Joinville and perpetuated in school texts, in which we learn of Louis' reaction to Joinville when the latter states that he would rather commit a mortal sin than contract leprosy. [34] This image of a man seemingly obsessed with sin, who offers to his friend a theoretical choice between two quite dissimilar things and then opts for what in the world's eyes is the less practical of the two (scolding his friend in the process for not having made the right choice), has contributed in no small way to the lingering image of Louis as an eminently impractical man. This impression can only be reinforced when we consider either the military disasters of the Seventh Crusade, during which Louis was taken prisoner and narrowly escaped death, or the almost total debacle of the Eighth Crusade, from which Louis did not return but upon which he embarked (at least in part) in the somewhat naïve hope of converting the Emir of Tunis.

---

[32] Wilhelm Berges, *Die Fürstenspiegel des hohen und späten Mittelalters* (Leipzig: Hiersemann, 1938), pp. 313-4.

[33] Ibid., pp. 301-2.

[34] Jean, Sire de Joinville, *Histoire de Saint Louis, le Crédo et la Lettre à Louis X*, éd. Natalis de Wailly (Paris: Le Clere, 1867), pp. 16-9.

It is not our intention here to try to dispel this image of the pious but slightly naïve monarch who would have preferred to be a monk if he could have had his way. When, however, we read the Instructions closely we learn how deeply committed Louis was to his beliefs. In perusing these paragraphs that he himself composed, the effect is somewhat different from the one produced by reading a pious and well-meaning account written about him. Whereas the latter often tends to be too saccharine or too didactic in tone, the former is astoundingly frank and direct; and while a biographer or chronicler can arouse in us intellectual reservations about the man since we might question the intentions of the writer himself, Louis is surprised here, so to speak, in the process of conversing with his daughter. And to the extent that a first person statement like this one, since it has no goal other than the one that prompted Louis to compose his text in the first place, has a more disarming and immediate effect on the modern reader, it helps to cast a more human and earthbound, but no less religiously committed, image of the man. Although the Instructions do faithfully reflect Louis' piety, they are nonetheless not the work of a totally impractical man.[35]

In the Instructions Louis gives careful and thoughtful articulation to his ideas on the relationship between the individual and God. After two introductory paragraphs, he begins by formulating what he takes to be the basis of the Christian life: disinterested love of God by the individual Christian. And since each person's moral conduct ought to be based on adherence to this premise, Louis will orchestrate the main points of his text around this conviction. He states directly to Isabelle (paragraph 3) his belief that one should not love God for the sake of any reward, earthly or otherwise, but rather for the sake of love itself, that is, in a selfless, idealistic way. But no matter how much self-interest is present to contaminate one's love of God, one can still be sure that if this love is displayed through a good life, a fitting reward will be

---

[35] It should also be noted that Louis addresses Isabelle with the formal *vous* while using the familiar *tu* with Philip. This use of *tu* by Louis with his oldest son and heir most likely reflects the intimacy in which father and son lived before Louis' death. On the other hand, since Isabelle was a Queen and a Countess living far away from her father, perhaps she deserved in her father's eyes the more formal *vous*.

forthcoming from God after death (4). This is so because in the past, through the incarnation, God first showed us his own unalloyed love for humankind by sacrificing his only son for our benefit (5).

Now having asserted the prime importance of unselfish love of God expressed through the living of a moral life, Louis proceeds to tell Isabelle how to live a good life so as not to be forgotten by God at the hour of death (6-9). First, one must do good and avoid evil in the form of mortal sin (6), even preferring to undergo bodily injury rather than commit a serious sin. More specifically, Louis writes of the need for frequent confession (and also how to choose a confessor, and to conduct oneself with the confessor), as well as of the utility of encouraging close friends to supplement the confessor's work by offering constructive criticism (7); the necessity of attending mass and other church services and how to conduct oneself during such ceremonies (one ought not talk in church, should pray both silently and in unison with others, and should strive to be especially devout during the consecration) (8); and finally, the usefulness of listening to sermons that are delivered either in public or in private session — but in the latter circumstance Isabelle is exhorted to allow herself to be sermonized only by truly religious people. And a last way to show this love of God — appended by Louis to this paragraph almost as an afterthought — is by purchasing indulgences (9).

In the next two paragraphs Louis changes his emphasis, departing from the general question of how the Christian should show his love for God, in order to delineate for Isabelle the ideal stance that should be assumed by her (and by any Christian) when confronted by the seemingly inscrutable inconsistencies of Providence. If things go badly and the outside world, the world of reality apprehended through the senses, sends affliction, then the first thing to do — and this is significant, is not to make pious gestures of resignation but to try to get good advice. For Louis, one should always strive to be rational in time of adversity and the process of meeting head on with a sometimes irrational world involves a cool acceptance of what is happening coupled with the good sense (should we say *mesure*?) to seek helpful and constructive advice. But if, says Louis, the problem in question still persists after having taken this step, then the thing to do is to put up with one's difficulty as best one can for in his opinion the reason why God allows people to suffer is because it is good for them — it makes them more worthy of heaven. But suffering is also something that people deserve, for when one considers all of one's past sins one realizes that any adversity one is called upon to suffer in life is small in comparison with the gravity of one's past offenses (10). If, on the other hand, God sends good fortune, Isabelle should immediately thank God for this generosity and be careful not to fall into a state of spiritual complacency, for nothing is worse in Louis' eyes than the use of one's God-given gifts for evil designs (11).

In the next two paragraphs Louis once again alters his focus slightly in order to deal specifically with the problem of interior psychological stress. Here he recognizes that the different masks that Providence wears can exercise varying stressful effects on the inner life of the individual Christian and because of this he repeats the advice given in paragraph 10: when suffering from mental or spiritual anguish Isabelle should consult her confessor or a friend in whom she has confidence, but she should take the latter course of action only if the nature of the problem is such that it can safely be divulged to another person (12). In paragraph 13 Louis turns the coin to show us its other face. Isabelle perhaps could be called upon by a friend to give advice or counsel and in Louis' opinion she should always be prepared to perform such a function for others, either by discreetly and charitably dispensing advice or, if need be, by offering a more concrete "aumosne" of some kind to the person in need (13).

In the last part of the main body of his text, Louis devotes five paragraphs to what we might call the subject of applied love in daily life, or Christian charity in action. In these paragraphs he no longer touches on the way Isabelle should react in unusual or demanding circumstances that are provoked either by the force of exterior events or by the interior stress of mental anguish. On the contrary, the emphasis here is on the mundane and the quotidian. He first calls for love of the poor and of people in religious life (14), but perhaps remembering his own predilection for the men of the mendicant orders, he counsels Isabelle to have a special consideration for people who have become poor voluntarily. Next he exhorts her to personally associate only with people of healthy moral repute — advice well given to a lady who was both a queen and a countess (15). He then goes on to advise obedience to husband, father and mother (16), and to counsel general good conduct in public life so that anyone who sees her or hears of her will never be able to say anything scandalous about her (17). Finally, in keeping with the longstanding Capetian tradition of relative moderation in dress, he repeats to her the sense of the famous statement to Joinville about how a "prud'homme" should dress. In a word, it is better to underdress than overdress (18).[36]

In paragraph 19 Louis begins his closing remarks by recalling the essence of the wisdom contained in paragraphs 3-5 in which he had admonished Isabelle to love God above all things. Here he once again denigrates the idea, common among Christians then and now, that good deeds should be done in order to merit the reward of heaven while evil ones should be avoided out of fear of punishment in hell. Only a disinterested love of God, says Louis, should motivate the Christian to seek perfection and avoid sin.

After making this final allusion to the importance of loving God, Louis ends by asking that masses be said in his honor after his death (20), by commanding Isabelle not to show the text of the Instructions to anyone else (21), and by wishing that God will grant her the grace to lead a good life — which to Louis' mind would enable her to demonstrate to God her love for him.

What we have here, if we look at the total structure of the work, is a logical, and in some areas, somewhat detailed prescription for the cultivation of the spiritual life. Louis' emphasis is of course on the interior life since he assumes that the life of the spirit is more real and important than mere physical existence. But in so far as the soul, the seat of one's consciousness, is anchored in the concrete and tangible reality of life, he also prescribes how Isabelle ought to strike a happy balance between the demands of each part of her nature. Thus, in opening the Instructions by exhorting her to love God for his own sake, Louis is emphasizing that the inner, spiritual reality of life is the point of departure from which should flow (and which should condition) all of one's outward conduct in the world. On the other hand, when he ends the work by making the wish that Isabelle will lead a good life, he is saying the same thing but from just the opposite point of view: the good life, in Louis'

---

[36] Ibid., pp. 16-7.

view, is one that must be based on faith and for this reason it is no more than the external sign that Isabelle does appreciate the importance of God in her life and is ordering her existence accordingly.

Louis is radically Augustinian in his acceptance of the primacy of the reality of the inner life. But this is only one of two presuppositions on which the text of the Instructions is built. The other is a temporal one, presented at the outset in paragraph 3, in which he reminds Isabelle that the Christian who leads a good life will be rewarded in the future (with a happy sojourn in heaven for eternity) because, *in the past,* God sacrificed his only son for humanity. In a single stroke, past and present, finite human history and man's hope for eternity, are linked. And it is this Christian view of human history, coupled with the necessity of loving God for his own sake, that immediately confers upon the Instructions a deep spiritual content they would not otherwise possess.

It is only after having established this groundwork that Louis proceeds to tell Isabelle that the best way to cultivate the inner life — and thereby qualify for the extra-temporal reward of eternity in heaven — is to take advantage of the various means through which the church dispenses divine grace (6-9). Building on this foundation, he next points out to her that no matter what befalls her, good or evil, it really does not make any difference as long as she confronts the inconsistencies of Providence with an appropriate attitude (10-11). On the other hand, given the prime importance attached to the inner life, Isabelle must be ready to meet any adversity that wells up from within her very being (12) and also make herself available to counsel friends who suffer from the same type of inner spiritual anguish (13). In other words, the outer and inner realities are presented here once again (10-13) and no matter what happens in life, good or evil, and no matter what its source, outward reality or inner stress, Isabelle should always be ready to meet it and accept it with a detachment firmly rooted in an absolute love of God.

The last five paragraphs of the main body of the text are addressed to Isabelle by Louis not as a spiritual adviser to a spiritual charge, but as a father to a daughter. Each one is eminently practical and vividly reflects realities of Louis' own life: love poor people; only admit spiritually healthy people into your personal entourage; develop filial attachment to husband, father and mother; do not give scandal; and do not dress ostentatiously. But even here the practical and the concrete are important especially because they are outward manifestations of an inner conviction and commitment (disinterested love of God) and are part of the divine plan through which human acts made in temporal history (beginning with Christ's death on the cross) have a supernatural value redeemable at death for an eternity of happiness in heaven. And each of these acts, says Louis, can be considered as a manifestation of the "good life." Thus, when he ends by wishing that "Nostre Sire vous fache bone en toutes coses," his assumption is that these acts will be an outward reflection of an inner love of God.

The Instructions to Isabelle are not original, nor are they overpowering in their impact on a modern reader. But when we look at this text closely, as we have done, we see that the Instructions are indeed well thought out and that they reflect an eloquent and succinct statement of high ideals on the part of the man who was the living moral force of Western Christendom at what might well have been its high point in medieval times.[37] The Instructions, with their companion text, the Teachings to Philip, capture the very essence of the radical otherworldliness of Louis and in so doing help us to understand that a realization of his wholehearted love of God above all things must be the cornerstone to our understanding not only of his writings, but of his whole life.

---

[37] Two recent books, by their very titles, attest to the growing scholarly awareness that Louis IX splendidly epitomizes the highest moral aspirations of his age. See Paul Labal, *Le Siècle de Saint Louis* (Paris: Presses Universitaires de France, 1972), and Régine Pernoud, *Le Siècle de Saint Louis* (Paris: Hachette, 1970).

Chapter VI

THE INSTRUCTIONS TO ISABELLE

When Paul Viollet first studied one of the four texts of the Saint-Pathus version of the Instructions in comparison with the texts found in B.N. ms. fr. 25462 (G) and B.N. ms. fr. 22921 (M),[1] he judged that the text of G was the best of the three. He did so because he felt that the Saint-Pathus text was slightly Latinized and because the text of M was not as old as that of G. Unfortunately, not only did Viollet make no attempt to offer a critical edition of the text of G, he also made no attempt to date the text. He wrote simply: "J'ajouterai, pour compléter ces renseignements, que le ms. N. D. 272 [our text of G] est l'œuvre d'un copiste picard qui écrit *chou* pour *ce*, *cose* pour *chose*: cela défigure légèrement la langue de saint Louis, très régulière, d'ailleurs, dans cet ancien manuscrit. J'ai eu sous les yeux un troisième manuscrit, celui de Saint-Victor 886, aujourd'hui no. 22921 du fonds français [our text of M]. C'est le texte de N.D. 272 en un langage un peu plus moderne: le manuscrit Saint-Victor a été éxécuté au XIVe siècle."[2] Referring to G as an "ancien manuscrit" is the closest that Viollet came to dating this text.

---

[1] See above, pp. 17-19. The text of the Guillaume de Saint-Pathus version that Viollet compared to G and M is not the one later chosen by Delaborde for his critical edition of the Saint-Pathus *Vie de Sant Louis*. Delaborde chose A whereas Viollet had used B. Delaborde rejected B as his base text because he considered it to be a copy of A. Finally, Viollet seems to have been unaware of the texts of the Instructions found in K and N.

[2] Paul Viollet, "Note sur le véritable texte des Instructions de Saint Louis à sa fille et à son fils Philippe le Hardi," *BECh*, XXX (1869), 134.

When, in 1933, Léon Levillain made his study of the text of the Instructions found in G, he concluded that "l'écriture est de la fin du XIIIe siècle ou des premières années du XIVe." [3] Obviously, Levillain is more precise in his dating of the text, but there is still a third, more detailed analysis of G. Immediately following the texts of the Teachings and Instructions in B.N. ms. fr. 25462, we find a text of the 13th century prose novella *La Fille du comte de Ponthieu*. [4] When Clovis Brunel edited the work in 1923, he felt impelled to write at some length of this manuscript since it contains the only Old French text of the work.

> ...c'est par un manuscrit unique, le numéro 25462 du fonds français de la Bibliothèque nationale qu'est connue la plus ancienne narration de la légende. Ce livre de petit format a été folioté au XVIe siècle. Sa reliure actuelle, assez grossière, paraît dater de deux siècles plus tard. Il est composé de deux parties. La première a été écrite par une même main du dernier quart du XIIIe siècle. Elle comprend diverses œuvres morales, parmi lesquelles les poèmes du Reclus de Molliens, le *Regret Notre-Dame*, l'*Ordre de chevalerie*, les *Enseignements de saint Louis*. La seconde est constituée par deux cahiers, l'un de quatre, l'autre de deux doubles feuillets. Elle se distingue de la partie précédente par la composition des cahiers, l'écriture, qui reste d'ailleurs du même temps, l'encre et l'ornementation. [5]

This third testimony regarding the probable date of our text agrees with our own judgment but, as we stated above (see pp. 59-62), the text of the Instructions found in G could not have been composed before 1297 because in the introduction to the text the scribe writes: "Chi apres sunt escrit li enseignement ke li bons rois sains Loÿs escrist de sa main a ma dame Ysabel, sa fille, qui fu roine de Navarre." Since Louis IX only became "sains Loÿs" in 1297, we estimate that our text dates from the very end of the 13th century or from the early years of the 14th century. [6]

---

[3] Léon Levillain, "Discours de M. Léon Levillain, Président de la Société, pendant l'exercise 1932-33," *ABSHF*, LXX (1933), 81.

[4] *La Fille du comte de Ponthieu*, éd. Clovis Brunel (Paris: Champion, 1923).

[5] Ibid., pp. IX-X.

[6] Op. cit., Henri Omont, *Bibliothèque Nationale, Catalogue Général des*

In composing the following critical edition of the Instructions, we have striven to remain as faithful as possible to the text of G, emending it only in those cases in which it is clearly in error and/or in which other texts furnish a reading that is clearly superior. Despite the fact that the text is composed in a *picard* dialect whose regional inflection and orthography were slightly different from those used by Saint Louis, we still consider this text to be the one that brings us the closest to Saint Louis' holograph.

Manuscrits Français; Anciens Petits Fonds Français, 3 vols. (Paris: Leroux, 1897-1902). II, 602-4. We recall that Omont dates B.N. ms. fr. 25462 from the 13th century.

CHI APRES SUNT ESCRIT LI ENSEIGNEMENT KE LI BONS ROIS SAINS LOŸS ESCRIST DE SA MAIN A MA DAME YSABEL, SA FILLE, QUI FU ROINE DE NAVARRE[1]

// 1   A sa chiere et amee fille Ysabel,[2] roine de Navarre, salus et amistié de pere.[3]

2   Chiere fille, pour che que je quit ke vous retenrés plus volentiers de moi[4] pour l'amour que vous avés a moi,[5] que vous ne feriés de pluisours autres,[6] j'ai pensé ke je vous fache aucuns enseignemens escris de ma main.[7]

3   Chiere fille, je vous enseigne que vous amés Nostre Signeur[8] de tout vostre cuer et de tout vostre pooir, car sans chou nus ne puet riens valoir.[9] Nule cose ne puet estre amee ne si droiturierement ne si pourfitablement.[10] Ch'est li sires a qui toute creature puet dire: "Sire, vous estes mes Diex. Vous n'avés mestier[11] de nus de mes biens." Chou est li sires qui envoia son fill[12] en terre et le livra a mort pour nous delivrer de la mort d'infer.[13]

4   Chiere fille, se vous l'amés, li pourfis en sera vostres. Mout est la creature desvoiie[14] qui aillors met l'amour de son cuer[15] fors en lui ou desous lui.

5   Chiere fille, la mesure dont nous le devons amer,[16] si est l'amer[17] sans mesure. Il a bien deservi que nous l'amons car il nous ama premiers.[18] Je vaurroi[19] ke vous seussiés bien penser as œvres ke li benois Fius Diu[20] fist pour nostre raenchon.

6   Chiere fille, aiiés grant desirier[21] coument // vous li puissiés plus plaire et metés grant entente[22] a eschiver toutes les coses que vous quideres[23] qui li doient desplaire. Especiaument vous

devés avoir cheste volenté que vous ne feriés [24] pechié mortel pour nule cose [25] qui peüst avenir, et ke vous vous laisseriés [26] anchois tous les membres trenchier et la vie tolir [27] par cruel martire que vous le [28] fesissiés [29] a ensient.

7   Chiere fille, acoustumés vous a souvent [30] confesser et eslisiés tous jours confessours qui soient de sainte vie et de souffissant lettreüre [31] par qui vous soiiés ensignie [32] des coses que vous devés eschiever et des coses ke vous devés faire. [33] Et soiiés de tel maniere par quoi vostre confessours et vostre autre [34] ami vous osent hardiement [35] ensignier et reprendre.

8   Chiere fille, oiiés volentiers le service de sainte Glise, [36] et quant vous serés u moustier, gardés vous de muser et de dire vaines [37] paroles. Vos orisons dites en pais ou par bouche ou par pensee, [38] et especiaument entrués con [39] li cors Nostre Signour Jhesu Cris [40] sera presens a la messe, soiiés plus en pais et plus ententieve a orison, et une pieche devant. [41]

9   Chiere fille, oiiés volentiers parler de Nostre Signour [42] en sermons et en privés parlemens. [43] Toutevoie privés parlemens // *203 v.* eschivés [44] fors que de gens [45] mout esleues en bontés et en sainteés. [46] Pourcachiés volentiers [47] les pardons.

10   Chiere fille, se vous avés aucune persecucion ou de maladie ou d'autre cose en quoi vous ne puissiés [48] metre conseil en bone maniere, souffrés le debonairement et en merchiiés [49] Nostre Signeur et l'en sachiés bon grei. Car vous devés quidier ke ch'est [50] pour vostre [51] bien et devés quidier [52] que vous l'aiiés deservi [53] et plus se il vausist, [54] pour chou que vous l'avés pau amé et pau servi et avés maintes coses faites [55] contre sa volenté.

11   Se vous avés aucune prosperité ou de santé de cors ou d'autre cose, [56] merchiiés ent [57] Nostre Signeur humelement et l'en sachiés bon grei ; et vous prenés bien garde que de chou n'empiriés ne par orgueil ne par autre mesprison, car chou est mout grans pechiés de guerroiier Nostre Signour [58] pour l'ocoison de ses dons.

12   Se vous avés aucune mesaise de cuer, [59] dites le a vostre confessour ou a aucune autre personne ke vous quidiés [60] qui soit loiaus et ki vous doive [61] bien cheler, pour chou ke vous le portés [62] plus en pais, se ch'est cose ke vous puissiés dire. [63]

13   Chiere fille, aiiés le cuer piteus [64] vers toutes gens ke vous entenderés [65] qui soient [66] a meschief ou de cuer // ou de cors et les secourés volentiers ou de confort ou d'aucune aumosne, selonc chou ke vous le porrés faire [67] en bone maniere.

204 r.

14   Chiere fille, amés toutes [68] bones gens, soient de religion, soient du siecle, [69] par qui vous entenderés ke Nostres Sires soit honnerés et servis. [70] Les povres amés et secourés, [71] et especiaument cheus qui, [72] pour l'amour Nostre Signour, se sunt mis a povreté.

15   Chiere fille, [73] prenéz vous garde a vostre pouoir que les femmes et l'autre mesgnie [74] qui repairent plus souvent et plus secretement avec vous soient de bone vie et sainte, et eschivés a vostre pouoir toutes gens de malvaise [75] renommee.

16   Chiere fille, obeïssiés humelement a vostre marit et [76] a vostre pere et a vostre mere es coses qui sunt selonc Dieu. Vous devés chou volentiers faire [77] pour l'amour que vous avés a aus [78] et assés plus pour l'amour Nostre Signour [79] qui ensi l'a ordené a cascun [80] selonc chou qu'il affiert; contre Dieu vous ne devés a nului obeïr.

17   Chiere fille, metés grant paine [81] que vous soiiés si [82] parfaite en tout bien [83] que chil qui orront parler de vous et vous verront i puissent prendre bon example. [84]

18   Il me samble qu'il est [85] bon ke vous n'aiiés [86] mie trop grant sourcrois de reubes ensamble ne de joiaus [87] selonc l'estat ou vous estes; ains [88] me samble miex que vous [89] fachiés vos ausmosnes au mains [90] de chou qui trop seroit, et me samble qu'il est bon que vous ne metés [91] mie trop grant tans ne trop grant estuide en vous parer ne achesmer. [92] Et prenés garde que vous ne fachiés outrage [93] en vostre atour, [94] mais tous jours vous enclinés // anchois devers le mains que devers le plus. [95]

204 v.

19   Chiere fille, aiiés un desirier en vous [96] ki [97] jamais ne se departe de vous, [98] ch'est a dire comment vous puissiés [99] plus plaire a Nostre Signour, et metés vostre cuer a chou ke se vous estiés chertaine que vous ne fuissiés jamais guerredounee de bien que vous fesissiés ne punie de mal que vous fesissiés, [100] si vous devriés vous garder de faire cose [101] ki despleüst a Nostre Signeur, [102] et entendre [103] a faire les coses qui li plairoient, a vostre pooir, purement pour l'amour de lui.

20   Chiere fille, pourcachiés volentiers orisons de bones gens et m'i acompagniés; [104] et se il avient [105] k'il plaise a Nostre Signour que jou trespasse de cheste vie devant vous, [106] je vous pri que vous pourcachiés messes et orisons et autres biens fais pour m'ame. [107]

21   Je [108] vous commant que nus ne voie chest escrit sans mon congiet, excepté vostre frere. [109]

22   Nostre Sire Diex vous fache bone en toutes coses [110] autant comme je desir [111] et plus assés ke je ne saroie desirrer. [112] Amen.

Chi finent li commandement ke li rois sains Loÿs fist a ma dame Ysabel, sa fille, qui fu roine de Navarre. //

VARIANTS

    E printed text of Latinized Saint-Pathus version
    G B. N. ms. fr. 25462 (base text for the present edition)
    K text presently located in Amiens Register AA4
    M B. N. ms. fr. 22921
    N B. N. ms. fr. 916

[1] *E* li benoiez sainz Loys envoia a ma dame Ysabel, sa fille, roine de Navarre, une letre d'enseignement escrite de sa propre main, de la quele... acion la teneur est tele; *K* Ch vecy les enseignemens de saint Loys qu'il fist a madame Yzabel, royne de Navarre, sa fille; *M* Ce sont les enseignemens que li bons roys saint Loys fist et escript de sa main et les envoya de Carthage ou il estoit a la royne de Navarre, sa fille; *N* Ce sont les enseignemens que le bon roy saint Loys fist et escript de sa main et les envoya de Carthaige ou il estoit a la royne de Navarre, sa fille. Et dit ainsi.

[2] *K* A sa chiere amie et fille Yzabel.

[3] *E* salut et amour de pere; *G adds* Ch; *K* salut de pere.

[4] *K* plus voulentiers de moy que d'un autre; *MN* plus volentiers et plus de cuer de moy.

[5] *MN* pour l'amour que vous y avez.

[6] *E* que vous ne feriez de aucuns autres; *K omits* que vous ne feriés de pluisours autres.

[7] *E* je pense que je vous ferai aucuns enseignemenz escris de ma propre main; *K* j'ay pensé que je vous face aucuns enseignemens de ma main.

[8] *E* Nostre Seigneur Dieu.

[9] *E* car sanz ce ne puet nul valoir nule chose; *K* car sans ce ne poeut riens valoir.

[10] *E* ne autre chose ne puet estre amee si profitablement; *G* Nule cose ne puet bien estre amee ne si droiturierement ne si pourfitablement; *K* ne nulle chose ne poeut estre amee si droturierement ne si proffitablement.

[11] *E* qui n'avez besoing.

¹² *E* son benoiet fuiz; *K* son cher fil.
¹³ *E* poines d'enfer; *K* paine d'enfer.
¹⁴ *E* mout hors voie; *K* desvoyee; *MN* deceue.
¹⁵ *E* qui met ailleurs l'amour de son cuer; *K* qui ailleurs met sa pensee et son coeur; *MN* qu ailleurs met son cuer ne sa cure.
¹⁶ *E* par la quele nous devons Dieu amer; *K* dont vous le devez amer.
¹⁷ *G* si est amer.
¹⁸ *EMN* premierement.
¹⁹ *KMN* vodroye bien
²⁰ *K* le benoit filz; *MN* le benoit filz de Dieu.
²¹ *EK* desir; *MN* grant desirier de savoir et de faire.
²² *E* grant cure et grant diligence.
²³ *K* cuidez.
²⁴ *K* ferez; *MN* faciés.
²⁵ *EMN* pour chose; *K* pour nulle rien.
²⁶ *E* souferriez; *K* laisserez.
²⁷ *E* ainçois que l'en vus trenchast touz les membres et que l'en vos ostast la vie; *G* anchois les membres cauper u detrenchier et la vie tolir; *K* avant tous les membres trencher et la vie tollir; *M* aincois touz les membres trenchier et la vie toulir; *N* aincois devez tous vous membres laisser trancher.
²⁸ *E* pechié mortel.
²⁹ *N* que le fere.
³⁰ *E* a confesser vos souvent; *G* souvent a; *K* a souvent; *MN* a vous confesser souvent et eslire.
³¹ *E* qui soit soufisamment letré; *G* de soufissant lettrure; *K* de souffissant lettreüre; *M* de souffisant lettreüre; *N* lettree.
³² *G* ensignie et doctrinee.
³³ *E* es choses que vous devez eschiver et que vous devez faire; *K* des choses que vous devez faire et que devez eschever; *M* des choses que vous devez faire.
³⁴ *K* voz autres bons amis; *M* vostre ami; *N* voz ami.
³⁵ *G omits* hardiement, *given by EKMN*.
³⁶ *M* oyés volentiers et soingeusement le service de sainte Eglise.
³⁷ *K* malvaises.
³⁸ *E* par bouche et par pensee; *K* ou de coeur ou de bouche ou en pensee.
³⁹ *E* quant; *K* tandis que; *MN* tant come.
⁴⁰ *E* li cors Jhesu Criz; *MN* le corps Nostre Seigneur.
⁴¹ *MN* devant la consecration.
⁴² *EMN* de Dieu.
⁴³ *E* et en parlemenz privez; *K* et divers parlemens.
⁴⁴ *E* mes eschivez touzjours privez parlemenz; *K* Eschevez compaignies; *N omits*.
⁴⁵ *EKM* fors de gens; *N omits*.
⁴⁶ *K* gens mout eslevees en sainteté et en bonté; *M* gens moult esleuz en Dieu en bonté et en sainteté; *N* gens de sainte vie.
⁴⁷ *E* Procurez volentiers indulgences et pardons; *M* porchaciez volentiers pardons et oroisons; *N omits*.
⁴⁸ *E* en la quele vous ne puissiez; *K* ou l'en ne puisse.
⁴⁹ *E* rendez pour ce graces; *K* et merchyés.
⁵⁰ *E* que il fet ce; *KMN* qu'il le face.
⁵¹ *E* nostre.
⁵² *E* et devez croire; *KMN* et devés penser.

⁵³ *EK* vous avez ce desservy; *M* vous avez tant et plus deservi; *N* vous avez tant plus deservi.
⁵⁴ *K* et autre chose s'il voulsist; *MN* se il voulsist.
⁵⁵ *E* fet mout de choses; *K* maintes choses dictes et faictes; *MN* maintes fois fait.
⁵⁶ *E* aucune prosperité de santé de cors ou autre; *K* aucunes prosperités de corps ou d'autres choses; *MN* aucune perversité ou deffaulte de corps ou de biauté ou d'autre chose.
⁵⁷ *EKMN* en.
⁵⁸ *E* c'est mout grant pechié que fere guerre a Nostre Seigneur.
⁵⁹ *E* tribulacion de cuer; *G* malaise de cuer ou d'autre cose; *KMN* mesaise de coeur. *Paragraph ten of the* Noster *ms. of the Teachings reads* mesaise de cuer.
⁶⁰ *E omits*; *MN* sachez.
⁶¹ *K* le vouldroit.
⁶² *E* pour ce que vous portez vostre tribulacion et soutiegniez plus en pes.
⁶³ *E* se ele est tele que vos la puissiez et doiez dire a vostre confesseur; *K* puissez fere; *MN* puissiez et doyés dire.
⁶⁴ *E* debonnere.
⁶⁵ *E* vers les genz que vos entendez; *K* vers gens que vous cuiderez; *MN* vers ceulz que vous entendrez. *Paragraph nine of the* Noster *ms. of the Teachings reads* envers touz ceus que tu cuideras.
⁶⁶ *EMN* sont.
⁶⁷ *E* selon ce que vos porrez; *MN* selon ce que faire le pourrez.
⁶⁸ *G* toutess.
⁶⁹ *E* et de religion et de siecle; *K* soient de religion soit de siecle; *MN* soient de religion ou seculiers.
⁷⁰ *K* servy et honnouré.
⁷¹ *E* Amez les povres et les secourez; *K* Et les povres secourez.
⁷² *K* ceulx qui pour l'amour de Dieu Nostre Seigneur Jhesu Crist et en ensuivant son commandement ont tous leurs biens habandonné et se sont mis a povreté.
⁷³ *G omits paragraph fifteen, the text of which is based on MN* (E).
⁷⁴ *E* pourveez vous a vostre pooir que les femmes et les autres mesniees qui avecques vous conversent plus priveement et secreement soient de bonne vie et de sainte; *K* prenez vous garde a vostre povoir que les femmes et l'autre mesquine qui plus secretement repairent avec vous soient de bonne et sainte vie; *M* prenez vous garde de vostre povoir que les femmes et l'autre mesgnie qui repairent plus souvent et plus secrettement avecques vous soient de bonne vie et sainte; *N* prenez vous garde a vostre povoir que les femmez et l'autre mesnie qui repairent plus souvent et plus secretement avec vous soient de bonne vie et sainte.
⁷⁵ *E* male.
⁷⁶ *K* a vostre mary, a vostre pere.
⁷⁷ *E* Vos devez volentiers faire a chascun ce qu'a lui apartient; *MN* Car ce devez vous volentiers faire.
⁷⁸ *E* pour l'amour que vous devez avoir; *KM* pour l'amour que vous devez avoir a eulz; *N* pour l'amour de Nostre Seigneur.
⁷⁹ *K* l'amour de Dieu Nostre Seigneur.
⁸⁰ *E* a ce einsi ordené; *K* ansi l'a ordonné.
⁸¹ *E* si grant entente; *K* paine.

82 *K* que vous soyés parfaitte.
83 *G omits* en tout bien, *given by EMN*; *K* en tous biens.
84 *E* que cil qui vous verront et orront parler de vous i puissent prendre bon essample; *K* et ce qui vous verront ou orront parler de vous, ilz puissent prendre prendre bon exemple; *MN* que ceulz qui vous verront et qui orront parler de vous y puissent prendre bon exemple.
85 *E* ce soit; *K* il fust; *MN* il seroit.
86 *KMN* n'eussiez.
87 *E* seurcrois de robes ensemble et de joiaus; *K* surcrois de robes ne de joyaux; *MN* secours ensemble de robes et de joyaux.
88 *MN* mais.
89 *E* vous en faciez; *K* vous en facez.
90 *MN omit* au mains.
91 *E* Et m'est avis que ce soit bon que vous ne metez; *G* et que vous ne metés; *K* et me semble qu'il fust bon que vous ne meissiés; *MN* Et me semble que il est bon que vous ne mettez.
92 *E* pas trop grant tens ne trop grant estude a vous parer et atorner; *K* ja trop grant temps a vous parer ne trop grande estude a vous acesmer; *M* ja trop grant temps ne trop grant estude a vous parer ne acesmer; *N* ja trop grant estude a vous parer ne acesmer.
93 *E* que vos ne faciez exces; *K* que vous ne facez ja nulle fois oultrage; *MN* que vous ne faittes nulle foiz oultrage.
94 *E* aournement.
95 *E* ainçois soiez plus encline au moins que au plus; *KMN* mais tous jours vous enclinez plus devers le moins (*K* mains) que devers le plus.
96 *K omits* en vous.
97 *EKM* qui; *N* que.
98 *E* de vos ne se parte; *K* ne se parte de vous; *MN* ne s'en parte de vous.
99 *K* c'est a dire comment vous devez; *MN* c'est comment vous puissiés.
100 *E* metez vostre cuer a ce que, se vous estiez certaine que vos n'auriez jamés guerredon de nul bien que vos feissiez, ne ne fussiez punie de mal que vous feissiez; *K* metez vostre cuer a ce que se vous estiez certaine que vous ne fussiez guerredonnee de bien que vous feissiez, *M* mettés vostre cuer a ce que se vous estiés certaine que vous ne fuissiés jamais guerredonnee de bien que vous feissiés, ne punie de mal que vous puissiés faire; *N* mettés vostre cuer a ce que se vous estiés certaine que jamais vous ne feussiés guerdonnee de bien que vous feissiez ne pugnie pour mal que vous peussiés faire.
101 *E* non pourquant si vos voudriez vous garder de fere chose; *MN* si vous devriés vous garder de pechier et de faire chose.
102 *E* Dieu.
103 *EKMN* entendriez.
104 *E* procurez volentiers les proieres des bonnes gens et m'acompaigniez a vous en ces proieres; *M* pourchaciez volentiers oroisons et prieres et bienz faiz des bonnes gens et m'i acompaigniés; *N* pourchaciés volentiers oroisons et prieres et biens fais des bonnes gens.
105 *K* et s'il advient chose qu'il plaise.
106 *E* que je me parte de cest monde ainçois que vous.
107 *E* l'ame de moi.
108 *KMN omit paragraph twenty-one.*

¹⁰⁹ *E* Je vous commant que nul ne voie cest escrit sanz mon congié, excepté vostre frere; *G* Je vous commant que nus ne voie chest escrit sans congiet.

¹¹⁰ *E* Nostre Sire vous face si bonne en toutes choses; *K* Nostre Seigneur Dieu vous face si bonne en toutes choses; *M* Nostre Sire Diex Jhesu Crist vous face si bonne; *N* Nostre Seigneur Jhesu Crist vous face si bonne.

¹¹¹ *EK* comme je desire; *MN* comme mon cuer le desire.

¹¹² *E* que je ne sache desirrer; *K* que je ne desire; *MN* que je ne dy ne ne scay desirier.

Appendix

TWO FORGED TEXTS OF THE INSTRUCTIONS

We feel it is necessary to add an appendix to this study for there are two extant texts (one from the 14th century, the other from the 15th) that purport to contain a set of Instructions of Saint Louis to one of his daughters. As we mentioned above in Chapter II (see pp. 24-25), both Saint-Pathus and Beaulieu mention other texts, aside from the one we have already presented, which were sent by Louis to Isabelle, probably during the period 1248-1254, while he was separated from his daughter. We recall that Beaulieu mentions that at some point during these years Louis sent "litteras speciales" to his daughter Isabelle. Since the description he gives of these "litteras speciales" does not coincide with our text of the Instructions, one is tempted to wonder whether one of these two remaining Middle French texts might reproduce distant ancestors of the original "litteras speciales." Likewise, when Saint-Pathus mentions that in addition to the text of the Instructions, Louis sent Isabelle "une letre escrite de sa main, en la quele il estoit... unes deceplines encloses," we cannot do otherwise but ask ourselves if one of these texts might produce for us a letter that originally accompanied a "deceplines" that Louis sent to his daughter.

The two texts in question are found in (1) B.N. ms. fr. 4977, fol. 73v.-74, and (2) Bibliothèque Royale Albert Ier, ms. 4373-76, fol. 139v.-151v. The first of these two texts, because of its handwriting and spelling, was most likely written in the 14th century and it paraphrases freely the genuine copy of the Instructions. The scribe, perhaps to hide the fact that he was doing no more than rewrite — in his own way — his model, alleges in his introductory paragraph that his text was originally written by Saint Louis for his youngest daughter Agnès who was born in 1257, married in 1279 to Robert II de Bourgogne and died in 1327. Presuming that the scribe was writing while Agnès was still alive, but after her marriage (in paragraph 19 he has Saint Louis speak to her of her children), 1279 would be the *terminus a quo* and 1327 the *terminus ad quem* for the composition of this forgery. And even if we were to take the scribe at his word and give credence to his assertion that Saint Louis actually did send a message to Agnès, this message would have had to be written between her birth in 1257 and his death in 1270. But since the scribe portrays Agnès as a married woman in this text, Saint Louis surely could not have been the author of the work for Agnès was not married until nine years after her father's death.

Unfortunately, this text is deciphered only with difficulty and in several places does not seem to make much sense. In fact, the editors of the *RHGF* felt so strongly that it was a forgery that they did not even bother to incorporate it in their compendium. In their opinion, the text is the work of "un clerc qui fait parler saint Louis, déjà couronné dans le ciel, en laissant voir clairement que cette œuvre est due tout entière à son imagination."[1] We basically agree with this assessment, but with the following reservation. The scribe's imagination does indeed play an important role in this text, but despite this fact one can still catch a glimpse of the model that he must have had before him. Thus, as our scribe invented a text of Instructions for Agnès, the original text of Instructions destined for Isabelle by her father (and we have no way of knowing which manuscript or combination of manuscripts of the Old French or Latinized version played the lead role) most assuredly served as a source of nourishment for our scribe's imagination.

The second of these two texts was published in Vol. 23 of the *RHGF* (1894), because the editors of the volume took it to be an authentic text originally authored by Saint Louis. Despite the fact that this text dates from the 15th century, is stylistically alien to Saint Louis' way of speaking and style of writing, and is addressed

---

[1] *RHGF*, XXIII, 131.

to "Sainte Geneviève," the editors argued that the work was a copy of an original that Louis must have dedicated to his daughter Marguerite. Earlier, Kervyn de Lettenhove had also taken the text to be authentic but had argued that it was originally composed by Saint Louis for his daughter Agnès.[2] This hypothesis was rejected by the editors for the following reason:

> S'il est vrai que saint Louis ait adressé quelques avis à la dernière de ses filles, Agnès, née au mois d'août 1260 [1257], il n'aura sans doute pas dit à une enfant de cet âge, de garder son cœur de toute ordure et de toutes mauvaises pensées, d'être souvent en oraisons et en larmes, de se croire toujours la pire femme de celles avec qui elle se trouvait, etc. De tels conseils étaient destinés à une femme déjà mariée, et Agnès ne le fut que sous le règne de Philippe le Hardi. Quant à Isabelle, reine de Navarre,

---

[2] Kervyn de Lettenhove, "Conseils de saint Louis à sa fille Agnès," *Académie Royale des Sciences, des Lettres et des Beaux-Arts de Belgique. Brussels. Commission Royale. Bulletins.* 2e série, XI (1858), 448-54. Lettenhove then changed his mind several years later. Although he became aware that B.N. ms. fr. 4977 was a forgery, he still considered Bibliothèque Royale Albert 1er, ms. 4373-76, to be authentic: "J'ai publié, il y a quelques années, des enseignements adressés par saint Louis à une de ses filles, enseignements qui ne devaient "estre monstrés mie a chascun" [ms. 4373-76 of the Bibliothèque Royale Albert 1er] et qui à ce titre paraissent être ignorés de ses contemporains. J'avais cru y reconnaître des conseils destinés à Agnès, depuis duchesse de Bourgogne, qu'il appelle dans son testament *carissima filia nostra*, et je me fondais sur l'existence dans la librairie de Charles V, d'un très petit livret "sans ais," intitulé: "Les enssengnemens Loys çai en aire roy de France à sa fille, la duchesse de Bourgogne." C'était une erreur. J'ai retrouvé à la Bibliothèque impériale de Paris, l'ouvrage mentionné dans l'inventaire de 1373, et intitulé: "Ce sunt les enseignemans que Loys çai en aires roy de France envoia à Agnès, sa fille, duchesse de Bourgogne." C'est une exhortation offerte non par Louis IX, mais sous son nom par quelque clerc à la duchesse de Bourgogne, après son mariage et avant la canonisation de son père, c'est-à-dire, entre les années 1275 et 1285 (sic). En voici l'*incipit*: "Loys, cay en airies roys dou réaume de France, louquel auqunes fois faillir convient, orandroit por le mérite de la mort Jhésu-Crit coronés ou réaume dou ciel qui faillir ne puet, à sa très-chière fille Agnès, duchesse de Bourgoine, salut et humblement despire ce mauvais monde laiant, et doucement desirier les consolations dou ciel." Il me reste à rechercher s'il ne faut pas plutôt attribuer à Blanche, seconde fille de saint Louis, l'honneur d'avoir reçu ces admirables conseils [found in ms. 4373-76 of the Bibliothèque Royale Albert 1er] restés inédits pendant six siècles." The above quote is from fn. 2 (pp. 300-1) of "Le Psautier de saint Louis," *Académie Royale des Sciences, des Lettres et des Beaux-Arts de Belgique. Brussels. Bulletins.* 2e série, XX (1865), 296-304.

elle a reçu de son père d'autres enseignements, qui sont depuis longtemps publiés. Restent donc Blanche et Marguerite, toutes deux nées en Palestine, à un an de distance, et mariées du vivant de saint Louis l'une à Ferdinand de la Cerda, l'autre à Jean Ier, duc de Brabant. L'instruction qu'on va lire leur convient également, et l'on pourrait même supposer que saint Louis l'adressa en même temps à l'une et à l'autre. Que s'il fallait faire un choix entre les deux, nous dirions que le nom de Marguerite, abrégé et à demi effacé, se serait prêté, plutôt que celui de Blanche, à la fausse lecture qui a trompé le copiste du XVe siècle. [3]

Given this background of scholarly acceptance of the text as an authentic one that reproduces an original by Saint Louis, we have edited it once again. We are in strong disagreement, however, with both Lettenhove and the editors of the *RHGF* regarding the authenticity of this work for it too is the creation of a scribe who most likely had access to a copy of the real Instructions to Isabelle and who, taking it as his point of departure, amplified and imagined as he saw fit. As we mentioned above, the very style and tone of the work are in complete disagreement with the way in which Saint Louis usually expressed himself in oral and written form. And when, in fact, Louis is made to say to his daughter "gardez vostre cuer de toute ordure," (paragraph 21, below), we have trouble imagining him writing a phrase like this for any one of his daughters, let alone for a young, unmarried one like Agnès. Likewise, when he is made to say that she should avoid sins of "lecherie" and "gloutonnie" (paragraph 2), it is our opinion that Louis just could not have written this text. In fact, this text is so obviously a 15th century forgery which, like the other forgery we are presenting here, was based in large part on a copy of the original Instructions to Isabelle, that we consider no further argument against its authenticity necessary. [4] An intelligent modern reader should have

---

[3] *RHGF*, XXIII, 131-2. We have consulted this manuscript and in our opinion "le nom de Marguerite" is not "abrégé et à demi effacé." Blanche (1253-1323) was married in 1269 and Marguerite (1254-1271) in 1270.

[4] Paragraph 31, below, in which Saint Louis is alleged to have written "Ne les monstrez mie a chascun, mais seul a seul les lisez," would seem to indicate that the forgery is based on a model which, like either G or E, expresses Louis' desire not to have the text of the Instructions become a public document.

no trouble recognizing it for the counterfeit that it is. Reproduction of both of these bogus texts in the same volume with our base text (G) of the real Instructions to Isabelle should be enough to prove the illegitimate paternity of both of them.

In conclusion, both texts are forgeries based ultimately on the real Instructions. Thus, in neither case can the texts we possess be said to represent those "litteras speciales" or any other missive that Louis wrote to Isabelle from abroad during the period 1248-54. But despite the fact that these texts represent ultimately no more than the imagination and good will of the men who created them, they do nonetheless point out that during the two centuries following Louis' death, people continued to be edified by his example. In particular, their existence shows that Louis was not only associated during these centuries with those values we usually impute to his life (fervor for the Crusades, charity, piety and humility), but also that he was taken as a writer of pious instructions who wrote for the benefit of children other than Philip and Isabelle. In this light then, we see that these texts vouch for a continuing interest in Saint Louis as a moral preceptor with a message still considered valid for succeeding generations. In the end, since both these texts are forgeries, this is the importance that we should attach to them.

FORGED TEXT OF THE INSTRUCTIONS FOUND IN B.N. MS. FR. 4977

// Ce sunt les enseingnemans que Loys caieneaires roys de France envoia a Agnes, sa fille, Duchesse de Bourgongne.

1   Loys caienaries[1] roys dou reaume de France louquel auqunes fois faillir convient orandroit por le merite de la mort[2] Jhucrit coronez ou reaume dou ciel qui faillir ne puet, a sa tres chiere fille Agnes, duchesse de Borgoine, salut.

2   Et humblement despire ce mauvais monde laians et doucement deserrer les consolacions dou ciel.

3   Se tu es biem amé lou monde et deserre ces honneurs, ces delis et ces richesses jusques au jour dui, saiches que tu es perdu tom tamps, qua ce ne puet longuemant durer. Ausimant si com dit Jeremies li prophetes: "Li mondes est ansi com la mauvaise famme, que celen que l'ame apovrit et puis tout, un le gete fors."[3]

4   Donc selonc le monde es biem amie, je te pri que ton cuer convertises am penser desormais ou sauvemant de t'ame en tel meniere que tu qui es partie de moy quant a la formacion[4] de ton cor avec moy puisses gloriousemant resuciter a la fin et de ta compaignie je me joïsse ou reaume dou ciel.

5   Pour ces chouses meaus faire, or presans escris te sera bailliés ou sunt contenus aucuns brief anseignemans les quex se tu fais, tu pués avoir certainne esperance de ton sauvemant.

6   Se tu ne les gardes tout, ou ne t'an tiens au plus pres que tu porres bonemant selonc ces condicions, ne croire personne qui t'esseguroit de ton sauvamant. Et mont fous est qui som estat ne met a segur.

173 v.

7   Au commancemant dois antandre que tant com vos estes en ce monde [5] non veant et esveugle, vos ne poés antandre riens des choses espiritues fors que em samblance des choses corpores.

8   Apres savoir dois que li cuers est li fontainne et cause de la voie corporex et est li mambres qui premiers vit et au dariens [6] muert.

9   Et pour ce je te descri les condicions natureux de ton cuer quant a som nom, quant a sa formacion, et quant es chouses qu'il [7] contient et quant a ses heuvres. Et selonc ce ausimant te descrivray les proprietés espiritues pour çou que miauz antandes et retenes quele [8] est vie de grace, laquelle tu dois mener. Et formoies en ton cuer plaim de vertuez, et ensit porres aver a la fin cuer de gloire renmply // es [9] cuers premieremant est ansit appellez pour cure et *174 r.* cusant que tu dois avoir.

10   Li cuers si est trop volaiges et ne l'am puet l'on tenir a um estat. Il est ausimant trop deserrés quar Deux le veut avor, deaubles le veut toure. Aprés il est en trop grant peril pour les temptacions de la char, dou monde, dou deauble. Et pour ce, tres grant diligence, cure, cusans, discrecions te convient avor se tu veus seguremant antre les perilz de ce monde.

11   Ceste vertus est approvee en saigemant ouvrer. Donques une partie de ton tamps dois determiner [10] a Deu en laquelle tu ne saches ne pansees fors ce qui appartient a Deu.

12   Et quanque tu es meffait es autres heuvres, adonques tu reprannes [11] devant li et l'an crie merciz et am bien avrac amandemant, soit de mauvaisses pansees [12] ou de queque autre chouses.

13   Auqune partie de tes [13] heuvres doivent ausimant estre an Deu devotemant prier.

14   Oïr devotemant sa parole quant tu poures lere au livre ce qui apartient a foy [14] quant te venra a point, et parler volontiers de lui en tous leus. Apres pansse diligaumant am tes beisoingnez.

15   Et quant tu avres tamps, ouvre de tes mains si com tu ses bien faire en tel maniere que tu ne soies oisouse. Et en toutes ces choses te garde de mauvaisses panssees.

16   Li tamps convenables pour panser an tes pechiez est devers le sor ou devers [15] le matin si com il te venra miauz a point. Et

garde que tous les sors tu t'endormes en bonnes pansees et aimes Deu quar mont de gans se sunt auqunes foys andormis en foles pansees de pechié et au matin ne se sunt pas trovez en vie mas au parfont d'anfer.

17   Li temps convenaubles pour panser a Deu et lui prier est quant l'on hout les messes et les autres houres dou jour. Et pour ces chouses faire, tu dois por tous leus avor oratoire secret. Et quant l'on fera le service de Deu, tu ne dois parler de besoingne temporel se ne est necessités.

18   Et queque besoingne que tu haes ou mains une messe completemant dois tu oïr chescom jour sans nulle autre besoing faire ne panser fors que a Deu.

19   Et ne dois pas sofrir que adonques venint vers toy ti anfans ou autres personnes, et amtandes au lour quant tu devraes panser a Nostre Seignour. Et saiches, se tu le fais autremant, tu poicheras griémant et mont en seres reprinse devant Deu.

20   Et quar mont de recreacions corporex convient panre pour hostel les henins [16] de monde; an ce te garde d'oïr foules paroles dou dire, et de fous regars de personnes, et de pointures, quar ce sunt seotes envenimees que trespercent jusques au cuer.

Notes on the Text of B.N. ms. fr. 4977, fol. 73v.-74

[1] This word is underlined in the text, both here and above in the introductory paragraph. Two separate notes in the margin refer to the word. The first reads as follows: "Ce mot ne m'est pas connu. Et ne scay quelle etiquette ou titre il en veult donner au Roy." The second reads: "Je pense que ce mot tant controversé doit être pris et corrigé dans le sens de ça en arières. "We agree with this latter notation which is written in a modern (19th century or later) hand. The former note probably dates from the 16th or 17th century.

[2] This word is unclearly written between the lines.

[3] Jeremias, both in his *Prophecy* and in his *Lamentations*, likens his compatriots, in their relationship to Yahweh, to an unfaithful spouse. Although we have not been able to find a precise source for this quotation, the following verses from Jeremias, in which he compares the punishment inflicted by God on the people of Israel to that meted out to an unfaithful wife by an angry husband, give us an idea of that particular aspect of Jeremias' writings that must have inspired this quotation. *Prophecy*, II, 19-20: "Here is the very proof of thy wickedness, the measure of thy unfaithful-

ness... Thou wast off to play the wanton, the nearest hill top or secret forest for thy bower. Alas, vineyard of mine that I planted with such care, never a worthless shoot! How is it thou hast played me false, and art no vineyard of mine?" Prophecy, II, 36: "How light a woman thou art, ever at thy old ways!" Prophecy, III, 1-2: "And thou with many lovers hath played the wanton; yet come back to me, the Lord says, and thou shalt find welcome. Lift up thy eyes to the bare hills, and tell me, which of them has not been the scene of thy shame?" *Lamentations*, I, 7: "Heinously Jerusalem sinned; what wonder if she became an outlaw? How they fell to despising her when they saw her shame, that once flattered her! Deeply she sighed, and turned away her head."

4 *formcacion.*
5 *en ce vre monde.*
6 *daries.*
7 *qui.*
8 text unclear.
9 This word is indented several spaces at the top of the page. One gets the impression that the scribe lost his train of thought in moving from fol. 173 v. to 174.
10 *determner.*
11 One would expect a reflexive here.
12 *penses.*
13 Text unclear.
14 Text unclear.
15 *deves.*
16 Text unclear.

FORGED TEXT OF THE INSTRUCTIONS FOUND IN B.R. ALBERT 1er, MS. 4373-76

// S'enssuivent les enseignemens et les bons exemples que le bon roy de France, monseigneur saint Loys, envoya a sa fille Sainte Genevieve,¹ en luy priant moult doulcement qu'elle les volsist mettre en œuvre, et retenir a son pooir en son cœur, car grant prouffit luy en vienrroit, de corps et de l'ame, et a elle et a toutes celles qui voldront prouffiter et amer Dieu, Nostre Createur et Seigneur.   *139 v.*

1   Le premier:²

Celluy qui en la congnoissance de son createur veult pourfiter // doit premierement traveillier de tout son corps de congnoistre sa vie, car quant plus congnoist l'omme ou la femme la vie de soymeismes, tant s'approuche il plus de la congnoissance de son crea-   *140 r.*

teur. Pour ce convient tourner souvent chascun a lui, et rappeller son sens et son entendement des choses de dehors, et soy enclorre en son cuer.

2   La seconde chose est que l'on doit diligenment enquerir // *140 v.* sa vie et regarder son cuer, et encerchier quelz pensees, quelz affections et quelz desirs il a euz le jour, s'il s'est delictez en nesune chose contre Dieu, s'il est en nesungz esmouvemens d'orgueil ou de felonie, ou d'envie ou de lecherie, ou de gloutonnie ou de parresse.

3   Parresse est ung pechié qui retrait l'ame de bien faire. Et doit penser quant longuement il a demouré en mauvaises pensees et en mauvaises // voulentez, et aussi doit bien regarder et examiner *141 r.* la condicion de son cuer. Et doit apres regarder sa vie dehors, si comme tous ses fais, ses parolles, ses regards, ses alees, toutes ses euvres et tout son temp, et penser les biens que Dieu lui a fais et fait tous les jours, et regarder comment il l'ayme, comment il le sert, comment il le garde, comment il garde ses commandemens, et comment il les a gardez ou temps passé. // *141 v.*

4   Fille, quant vous levez au matin, et le horologe Dieu vous esveille, si gectez les yeulx de vostre cuer a vostre Dieu qui vous a fait, et lui recommandez vostre besongne; et lui priez qu'il vous gard de pechier, et proposez amendement de tous voz meffais, et de mener bonne vie.

5   Fille, quant vous estes ou moustier ou hors mostier pour dire vos heures et voz // oroisons, ayez vostre cuer a Dieu du tout, *142 r.* et ne vous souviengne de nesune vanité ne de nul pensement temporel; et en toutes voz euvres ayez vostre cuer ordonné a Dieu comme a cellui qui tout voyt.

6   Fille, quant vous venez a la table pour mangier, vous ne devez mie querre seulement le delict de la bouche, mais vostre soustenance, et penser a Dieu tant que vous ne prenez plus que vous ne devez. //

7   Fille, au lever de mengier vous devez rendre graces a Dieu, *142 v.* et prier pour ceulx de qui biens vous vienz, et prier Dieu qu'il vous pardoint.

8   Fille, se vous estes en compaignie ou parler vous conviengne, parlez par raison; et avant la parolle viengne a la bouche, deux foys devez penser parmy l'abyme de la raisson. //

9   Fille, se vous voulez parler a homme, mectez garde que vous ne dictes chose ou l'on puisse mal penser; mais dictes parolles qui touchent a bon ediffiement, par quoy on puist jugier que vous estes fille saige et bien advisee. *143 r.*

10   Fille, quant vous, apres complie au soir, vous voulez aler gesir, ainçois que vous vous couchiez, tenez chappictre de vous-meismes en vostre cuer // sans noyse, et appellez toutes voz pensees diligemment; et pensez se vous avez mespris le jour, ou en penser, ou en regarder, ou en veoir, ou en oÿr, ou en mal dire, ou autre mauvaise parolle, ou en mauvaises pensees, ne en desirer, ne en vouloir, ne en mauvaises euvres. Et a Dieu devez crier mercy, et espurgier vostre conscience par repentance de chascune deffaulte ou vous avez vostre createur courroucé. // *143 v.*

11   Fille, parlez en telle maniere que vostre parolle soit atrempee de la loy de charité, et que vostre parolle ne griefve a nulluy. *144 r.*

12   Fille, n'ayez nulle acointance a homme que vous ne sachiez qu'il soit en l'amour de Dieu et qu'il ne soit de bonne vie.

13   Fille, n'ayez nulle familliarité trop grant a nulle creature, // mais soyez franche de cuer et d'esperit. *144 v.*

14   Fille, soyez humble de cuer et d'abit, et priez pour le monde et quanques y a, car tout conviendra laissier.

15   Fille, si respondre vous convient a aucunes gens, si respondez simplement et a pou de parolles; et soyez // isnelle et appareillee a oÿr parler de Dieu, et recevez la bonne parolle pour vostre cuer nourir et pour vostre vie amender. *145 r.*

16   Fille, aymez povres gens, si vous aymera Dieu; et aymez toutes bonnes gens, si aurez part en leurs bontez.

17   Fille, toute familliarité vous desplaise; [3] especialement de // personne dont confusion vous peut venir; mais ayez Dieu en familliarité, et les benois angelz et les sains de paradis; si feront vostre besongne devant Dieu. *145 v.*

18   Fille, soyez simple et honneste et pou parlanz, de bonnes meurs et de bonne conversacion, et pensez tousdis que Dieu vous voyt. //

19   Fille, aymez saincte Eglise et jeusnez voulentiers; et quant vous y estes, si soyez close dehors et n'y parlez point; mais pensez *146 r.*

en vos deffaultes et en vostre Dieu qui est present, et lui monstrez vostre cuer.

20   Fille, pensez souvent a la mort et comment le corps pourrira, et tout fauldra, et conviendra mourir et compter // et paier. Ceste *146 v.* pensee vous fera haÿr pechié, et vous esmouvera de bien faire.

21   Fille, gardez vostre cuer de toute ordure et de toutes mauvaises pensees, et boutez arriere les temptacions de l'ennemy.

22   Fille, soyez debonnaire et souffranz, et ne retenez nulle yre en vostre cuer, mais pardonnez legierement. //

23   Fille, ne soyez mie voulentiers en compaignie noyseuse ne *147 r.* mal disant, et gardez vostre bouche de parler d'autruy en mal, et n'en oyez parler.

24   Fille, soyez souvent en oroisons et en larmes; car les oroisons sont les escus encontre les assaulx de l'ennemy, et reffuge en toutes tribulacions, et droite lumiere par laquelle l'ame scet ses deffaultes. //

25   Fille, soyez humble et pou vous prisez, et vous sembler *147 v.* tousdis que vous estes la pire femme de celles en la qui compaignie vous estes. Et soyez lye et joyeuse du bien de vostre proesme, et doulante de son dommaige et de son mal, et soyez piteuse aux povres gens, et ainsi aura Dieu pitié de vous.

26   Fille, soyez au matin esveillee pour vous commander a Dieu // et pour aler au moustier, ne ne passez jour que vous n'oyez *148 r.* messe, et oyez voulentiers parler de Dieu.

27   Fille, soyez veritable, et ne jurez point, ne mentez, ne ne parjurez; mais ayez tousdis verité en bouche, ordonnance en parolle, et parlez petit.

28   Fille, par voz dis ne nuisez a nulluy ne grevez; aussy // *148 v.* n'ayez voulenté de vous vengier, mais soiez paisible a toute maniere de gent.

29   Fille, aymez et honnourez Nostre Seigneur, et portez paix a tous ceulx qui demourreront avec vous.

30   Fille, ayez en vostre cuer la souvenance de la souffrance de vostre benoit doulx amy Jhesu Crist; car c'est une chose qui moult peut ung cuer // esmouvoir a Dieu mieulx aymer et a soy *149 r.*

garder de pechié, quant on regarde comment le doulx Jhesus s'abandonna a mort honteuse et douloureuse pour nous de pechié delivrer. C'est grant honte doncques de soy mectre si legierement a pechié, quant il le convient si chierement acheter.

31 Fille, entendez a ces enseignemens que je vous envoye, et vous ordonnez selon ce qu'ilz dient, // si menerez vie de preude *149 v.* femme et devote personne. Ne les monstrez mie a chascun, mais seul a seul les lisez, et vous y mirez et informez vostre vie, car c'est la voye de venir a Dieu.

32 Et puis devez dire ainsi et reclamer Nostre Seigneur Jhesu Crist: "O Dieu, qui m'as fait a t'ymaige et rachetee de ton precieux sang, et m'as // gardee en ma jeunesse, et attendu par ta saincte *150 r.* misericorde en mes pechiez, et donné de tes biens, et amenee a ton saint baptesme. Et par ta saincte doulceur et par les biens que tu m'as fais, et mil temps plus que je ne pourroie dire, je te pry que tu me doins pouoir de toy servir et aymer, et de moy garder de tous pechiez et aider en mes temptacions, et donner patience en mes // tribulacions, et pouoir et grace de tout bien faire en ceste mortel *150 v.* vie, et toy si amer et servir que je puisse apres toy venir a ton saint paradis. Amen" "Dieu Jhesu Crist, cui bontez on ne peut espuisier, cuy misericorde ne faillit oncques, qui tout et tous biens voulez, pardonnez moy mes pechiez, et me donnez grace // de moy amender, *151 r.* et de moy garder, et de vous aymer. Sire, je ne viens mie a vous en fiance de mes merites, mais en fiance purement de vostre saincte misericorde. Et se voz nom, Jhesus, en porte doulceur et pitié, faictes moy doncques misericorde et pitié; car se j'ay desservy dureté de mes pechiez et de mes maulx, que je recongnois[4] qui sont grans et abhominables devant vostre benoite face, si scay je de // certain que vous estes tres piteux, et avez tres plus grant talent *151 v.* du pardonner que les pecheurs de mercy crier. Pour ce vous prie feablement que vous ayez mercy de vostre creature qui retourne a vous de cuer contrict et repentant. Amen. Deo dicamus gratias. Pater noster et Ave Maria."

TWO FORGED TEXTS OF THE INSTRUCTIONS 99

Notes on the Text of Bibliothèque Royale Albert Ier, ms. 4373-76, fol. 139v.-151v.

[1] This word is underlined in the text. Saint Louis had no daughter named Geneviève.

[2] After his introductory paragraph, the scribe wrote "Le premier" in the middle of the page as if he intended to introduce each paragraph in this way. However, he does so only in this instance and abandons this procedure for all subsequent paragraphs, none of which is numbered.

[3] *desplaie*

[4] *je ne recongnois.*

BIBLIOGRAPHY

PRIMARY SOURCES:

Belloloco, Gaufridus de (Geoffroi de Beaulieu). *Vita et Sancta Conversatio Piae Memoriae Ludovici quondam Regis Francorum*, in *RHGF*, XX, 3-27.
Carnotensis, Guillelmus (Guillaume de Chartres). *De Vita et Actibus Inclytae Recordationis Regis Francorum Ludovici*, in *RHGF*, XX, 27-41.
Joinville, Jean de. *Histoire de Saint Louis*, ed. Claude Ménard, Paris, 1617.
———. *Histoire de Saint Louis, Credo et Lettre à Louis X*, ed. Natalis de Wailly, Paris, Le Clere, 1867.
———. *Histoire de Saint Louis, Credo et Lettre à Louis X*, ed. Natalis de Wailly, Paris, Firmin-Didot, 1874.
Nangioco, Guillelmus de (Guillaume de Nangis). *Chronicon*, in *RHGF*, XX, 543-82; *Vita Sancti Ludovici*, in *RHGF*, XX, 309-465.
Saint-Denis, Yves de. *Gesta Sancti Ludovici Noni Francorum Regis*, in *RHGF*, XX, 45-57.
Saint-Pathus, Guillaume de. *Vie de Saint Louis*, ed. H.-Fr. Delaborde, Paris, Picard, 1899; also in *RHGF*, XX, 58-121.
———. *Les Miracles de Saint Louis*, ed. Perceval B. Fay, Paris, Champion, 1931; also in *RHGF*, XX, 121-89.
Vignay, Jean du. *Chronique de Primat*, in *RHGF*, XXIII, 5-106.

SECONDARY SOURCES:

Artonne, André. "Le Recueil des traités de la France composé par ordre de Charles V," *Recueil de travaux offerts à Clovis Brunel*, 2 vols., Paris, Société de L'Ecole des Chartes, 1955. I, 53-63.
Beauvais, Vincent de. *De Eruditione Filiorum Nobilium*, ed. A. Steiner, Cambridge (Mass.), Mediaeval Academy of America, 1938.
Berger, Elie. *Histoire de Blanche de Castille*, Paris, Thorin, 1895.
Berges, Wilhelm. *Die Fürstenspiegel des hohen und späten Mittelalters*, Leipzig, Hiersemann, 1938.
Crist, Larry S. "The Legendary Crucifixion of Jehan Tristan, Son of Saint Louis," *Romania*, LXXXVI (1965), 289-306.
d'Arbois de Jubainville, M.-H. *Histoire des ducs et des comtes de Champagne*, 6 vols., Paris, 1859-66.
Delaborde, Henri-François. "Le Texte primitif des Enseignements de Saint Louis à son fils," *BECh*, LXXIII (1912), 73-100.

Delaborde, Henri-François. "Le Texte primitif des Enseignements de Saint Louis à son fils" (suite et fin), *BECh.*, LXXIII (1912), 237-62.
———. "Réponse de M. le Comte François Delaborde," *BECh*, LXXIII (1912), 502-4.
Duchesne, François. *Historiae Francorum Scriptores*, 5 vols., Paris, 1636-49.
Dusevel, H. "Enseignements de Saint Louis à madame Ysabel royne de Navarre, sa fille," *BSHF*, 2 août 1841, 128-30.
Foulet, Alfred. "Jehan Tristan, Son of Saint Louis, in History and Legend," *Romance Philology*, XII (1959), 235-40.
Gabriel, Astrik. *The Educational Ideas of Vincent of Beauvais*, Notre Dame (Ind.), The Mediaeval Institute, 1956.
Géraud, H. éd. *Chronique latine de Guillaume de Nangis de 1113 à 1300*, 2 vols., Paris, Renouard, 1843.
Gossen, Carl Theodor, *Grammaire de l'ancien picard*, Paris, Klincksieck, 1970.
Grémont, Bernard, "La Chronique d'Yves de Saint-Denis," (Thèse de l'Ecole des Chartes), *BECh*, CX (1952), 319.
Histoire Littéraire de la France, ouvrage... continué par des membres de l'Institut, 40 vols., Paris, 1824- .
Kervyn de Lettenhove, Joseph. "Conseils sur les devoirs des rois, adressés à Saint Louis par Guibert de Tournay," *Académie Royale des Sciences, des Lettres et des Beaux-Arts de Belgique. Brussels. Commission Royale d'Histoire. Bulletins.* Première Série, XX (1853), 496-505.
———. "Relation de la première croisade de Saint Louis, par Guibert de Tournay," *Académie Royale des Sciences, des Lettres et des Beaux-Arts de Belgique. Brussels. Commission Royale d'Histoire. Bulletins.* 2e Série, IV (1858), 250-64.
———. "Conseils de Saint Louis à sa fille Agnès," *Académie Royale des Sciences, des Lettres et des Beaux-Arts de Belgique. Brussels. Commission Royale d'Histoire. Recueil de ses Bulletins.* 2e Série, XI (1858), 448-54.
———. "Le Psautier de Saint Louis," *Académie Royale des Sciences, des Lettres et des Beaux-Arts de Belgique. Brussels. Commission Royale d'Histoire. Bulletins.* 2e Série, XX (1865), 296-304.
Langlois, Charles-Victor. *La Vie en France au moyen-âge*, 4 vols., Paris, Hachette, 1924-28.
Laubscher, G. G. *The Syntactical Causes of Case Reduction in Old French*, Princeton, Princeton University Press, 1921.
Le Nain de Tillemont, Louis Sébastien. *Vie de Saint Louis*, 6 vols., Paris, Renouard, 1847-51.
Levillain, Léon, "Discours de M. Levillain, Président de la Société," *ABSHF*, LXX (1933), 71-84.
Molinier, Auguste. *Les Sources de l'Histoire de France des origines aux guerres d'Italie*, 6 vols., Paris, 1901-1906.
O'Connell, David. *The Teachings of Saint Louis: A Critical Text*, Chapel Hill, University of North Carolina Press, 1972.
———. *Les Propos de Saint Louis*, préfacés par Jacques Le Goff, Paris, Gallimard, 1974.
Omont, Henri. *Bibliothèque Nationale, Catalogue Général des Manuscrits Français; Anciens Petits Fonds Français*, 3 vols., Paris, Leroux, 1897-1902.
Petit, Joseph. *Essai de restitution des plus anciens Mémoriaux de la Chambre des comptes de Paris*, intro. Ch.-V. Langlois, Paris, 1899, I-XXIII.

Recueil des Historiens des Gaules et de la France, éd. Bouquet, 24 vols., Paris, 1840-1904.

Riant, M. "Déposition de Charles d'Anjou pour la canonisation de Saint Louis," *Notices et Documents publiés pour la Société de l'Histoire de France,* Paris, 1884, pp. 155-76.

Thompson, James Westfall. *The Literacy of the Laity in the Middle Ages,* Berkeley, University of California Press, 1939.

Tournai, Guibert de. *Eruditio Regum et Principum,* éd. A. de Poorter, Louvain, Institut Supérieur de Philosophie, 1914.

Viard, Jules, éd., *Les Grandes Chroniques de France,* Paris, Klinksieck, VII (1932), X (1953).

Viollet, Paul. *Oeuvres chrétiennes des familles royales de France,* Paris, Poussielgue, 1870.

———. "Note sur le véritable texte des Instructions de Saint Louis à sa fille et à son fils Philippe le Hardi," *BECh,* XXX (1869), 129-48.

———. "Les Enseignements de Saint Louis à son fils," *BECh* XXXV (1874), 1-56.

———. "Les Enseignements de Saint Louis à son fils, Lettre à M. le comte François Delaborde," *BECh,* LXXIII (1912), 490-501.

Wailly, Natalis de. "Mémoire sur le *Romant* ou Chronique en langue vulgaire dont Joinville a reproduit plusieurs passages," *BECh,* XXXV (1874), 217-48.

ERRATA TO OUR EDITION OF THE TEACHINGS OF SAINT LOUIS

Paragraph
- 2: enseingnié (enseignié)
- 15: Nostre Sires (Nostre Seigneur)
- 16: juques (jusques)
- 18: prodommes (preudomes)
- 19: Nostre Sires (Nostre Seigneur)
- 19: saintte (sainte)
- 20: ceuz (ceus)
- 20: Nostre Sires (Nostre Seigneur)
- 21: conseulz (conseilz)
- 22: pour amour (par amour)
- 23: prodommes (preudomes)
- 24: trouver (trover)
- 24: ou forfet (en forfet)
- 24: maufeteur (maufetaur)
- 25: Seignieur (Seigneur)
- 26: autrui (autruy)
- 27: honneur (honeur)
- 28: osté (ostés)
- 29: Nostre Sires (Nostre Seigneur)
- 32: Seignieur (Seigneur)
- 33: honneur (honeur)

NORTH CAROLINA STUDIES IN THE ROMANCE LANGUAGES AND LITERATURES

I.S.B.N. Prefix 0-8078-

Recent Titles

RICHARD SANS PEUR, EDITED FROM "LE ROMANT DE RICHART" AND FROM GILLES CORROZET'S "RICHART SANS PAOUR", by Denis Joseph Conlon. 1977. (No. 192). -9192-4.
MARCEL PROUST'S GRASSET PROOFS. *Commentary and Variants*, by Douglas Alden. 1978. (No. 193). -9193-2.
MONTAIGNE AND FEMINISM, by Cecile Insdorf. 1977. (No. 194). -9194-0.
SANTIAGO F. PUGLIA, AN EARLY PHILADELPHIA PROPAGANDIST FOR SPANISH AMERICAN INDEPENDENCE, by Merle S. Simmons. 1977. (No. 195). -9195-9.
BAROQUE FICTION-MAKING. A STUDY OF GOMBERVILLE'S "POLEXANDRE", by Edward Baron Turk. 1978. (No. 196). -9196-7.
THE TRAGIC FALL: DON ÁLVARO DE LUNA AND OTHER FAVORITES IN SPANISH GOLDEN AGE DRAMA, by Raymond R. MacCurdy. 1978. (No. 197). -9197-5.
A BAHIAN HERITAGE. An Ethnolinguistic Study of African Influences on Bahian Portuguese, by William W. Megenney. 1978. (No. 198). -9198-3.
"LA QUERELLE DE LA ROSE: Letters and Documents", by Joseph L. Baird and John R. Kane. 1978. (No. 199). -9199-1.
TWO AGAINST TIME. *A Study of the very present worlds of Paul Claudel and Charles Péguy*, by Joy Nachod Humes. 1978. (No. 200). -9200-9.
TECHNIQUES OF IRONY IN ANATOLE FRANCE. Essay on *Les sept femmes de la Barbe-Bleue*, by Diane Wolfe Levy. 1978. (No. 201). -9201-7.
THE PERIPHRASTIC FUTURES FORMED BY THE ROMANCE REFLEXES OF "VADO (AD)" "PLUS INFINITIVE, by James Joseph Champion. 1978 (No. 202). -9202-5.
THE EVOLUTION OF THE LATIN /b/-/ʉ/ MERGER: A Quantitative and Comparative Analysis of the B-V Alternation in Latin Inscriptions, by Joseph Louis Barbarino. 1978 (No. 203). -9203-3.
METAPHORIC NARRATION: THE STRUCTURE AND FUNCTION OF METAPHORS IN "A LA RECHERCHE DU TEMPS PERDU", by Inge Karalus Crosman. 1978 (No. 204). -9204-1.
LE VAIN SIECLE GUERPIR. A Literary Approach to Sainthood through Old French Hagiography of the Twelfth Century, by Phyllis Johnson and Brigitte Cazelles. 1979. (No. 205). -9205-X.
THE POETRY OF CHANGE: A STUDY OF THE SURREALIST WORKS OF BENJAMIN PÉRET, by Julia Field Costich. 1979. (No. 206). -9206-8.
NARRATIVE PERSPECTIVE IN THE POST-CIVIL WAR NOVELS OF FRANCISCO AYALA "MUERTES DE PERRO" AND "EL FONDO DEL VASO", by Maryellen Bieder. 1979. (No. 207). -9207-6.
RABELAIS: HOMO LOGOS, by Alice Fiola Berry. 1979. (No. 208). -9208-4.
"DUEÑAS" AND "DONCELLAS": A STUDY OF THE "DOÑA RODRÍGUEZ" EPISODE IN "DON QUIJOTE", by Conchita Herdman Marianella. 1979. (No. 209). -9209-2.
PIERRE BOAISTUAU'S "HISTOIRES TRAGIQUES": A STUDY OF NARRATIVE FORM AND TRAGIC VISION, by Richard A. Carr. 1979. (No. 210). -9210-6.
REALITY AND EXPRESSION IN THE POETRY OF CARLOS PELLICER, by George Melnykovich. 1979. (No. 211). -9211-4.
THE FICTIONS OF THE SELF. THE EARLY WORKS OF MAURICE BARRES, by Gordon Shenton. 1979. (No. 214). -9214-9.
CECCO ANGIOLIERI. A STUDY, by Gifford P. Orwen. 1979. (No. 215). -9215-7.
THE INSTRUCTIONS OF SAINT LOUIS: A CRITICAL TEXT, by David O'Connell. 1979. (No. 216). -9216-5.

When ordering please cite the *ISBN Prefix* plus the last four digits for each title.

Send orders to: University of North Carolina Press
                  Chapel Hill
                  North Carolina 27514
                  U. S. A.

The Department of Romance Studies Digital Arts and Collaboration Lab at the University of North Carolina at Chapel Hill is proud to support the digitization of the North Carolina Studies in the Romance Languages and Literatures series.

www.ingramcontent.com/pod-product-compliance
Lightning Source LLC
Chambersburg PA
CBHW020421230426
43663CB00007BA/1260